Suzanne O'Hara established and heads the Moore (NI) LLP specialist SDLT advisory service which provides specialist property tax advice to solicitors, private clients, accountants & other professionals. Suzanne has been advising on UK tax matters for 15 years, solely concentrating on property tax matters in recent years.

Suzanne read Law and Accounting at Queen's University, Belfast. She is a Chartered Tax Adviser and also holds the Advanced Diploma in International Taxation, being awarded the Worshipful Company of Tax Advisers Medal for the highest marks in the Principles of Corporate and International Taxation paper. She also lectures for the Irish Institute of Tax on the Principles of International Tax and more recently for the Institute of Professional Legal Studies at Queen's University.

A Practical Guide to Stamp Duty Land Tax in England and Northern Ireland

A Practical Guide to Stamp Duty Land Tax in England and Northern Ireland

Suzanne O'Hara LLB (Hons), ATT, CTA, ADIT
Head of SDLT advisory service, Moore (NI) LLP

Law Brief Publishing

Published 2020 by Law Brief Publishing, an imprint of Law Brief Publishing Ltd
30 The Parks
Minehead
Somerset
TA24 8BT

www.lawbriefpublishing.com

Paperback: 978-1-913715-20-5

For Edith Coco. You'll never know, dear, how much I love you.

Preface

Since qualifying as a tax advisor, I have enjoyed finding ways in which to break down and explain complex matters. Those who have encountered me in a professional capacity will know that I am especially fond of drawing pictures to help explain difficult concepts; alas, this book has been spared my artistic endeavours. Colour is added, I hope, via an extensive selection of case studies.

In 2016, I discovered my favourite tax: SDLT, Henceforth, my working life (and sometimes my social life) has been centred on providing SDLT advice to solicitors, accountants, other professional and private clients. I consider myself quite privileged in this regard.

Every day I am asked to advise on areas of uncertainty as to how the SDLT legislation is applied; rightly so, it can be very complex. There are unlimited permutations of client-specific facts which can produce different outcomes in each individual case.

And hence the need for this book.

What I hope I have achieved is a book that can be picked up time and time again. A useful resource, that precludes the wading through text to reach a solution. Sometimes, however, in more complex scenarios, a deeper dive is unavoidable, and this is where an SDLT specialist should be called on. I have tried to identify such circumstances within this book.

I would like to thank my wonderful husband, family and friends, who have (as I have been writing this book) had to participate in many more SDLT-based conversations than the average layperson deserves. In addition, I would like to say a special thank you to Mr Nigel Thompson, who was my mentor in the early days as I learned about my favourite tax.

The law quoted is believed to be accurate at 23 July 2020.

I sincerely hope the reader finds this book useful.

Suzanne O'Hara
July 2020

How to Use This Book

Up until recently, SDLT was a pretty straightforward consideration. In the last few years, however, it has become an increasingly complex area and busy solicitors often have neither the time nor the inclination to delve into the fine print. A medical analogy might be apt. When it comes to SDLT, the role of the solicitor is akin to that of a GP; they have a huge knowledge of ailments and can cure most, but occasionally they'll have to refer to a specialist. This book will help with those quick diagnoses, whilst also signposting the appropriate time at which to call in the surgeon.

At the risk of exhausting the comparison, readers would do well to regard HMRC's SDLT calculator as the equivalent of googling one's own symptoms: you'll get a very broad set of results, which doesn't take into consideration the nuances of a specific case. The difference between that original calculation and an expert diagnosis can equate to tens, and in some cases, hundreds of thousands of pounds.

The first part of the book takes the reader step-by-step through the early parts of the SDLT legislation. These are the steps at which the practitioner will confirm that there is indeed a reportable transaction, how much to report and what rate to apply.

In the view of the author, it is important to take a systematic approach and work through the early provisions in the legislation first; this will ensure that land transactions that are within the scope of SDLT are correctly identified and reported (and, by the same token, that land transactions which fall outside the scope are not reported and taxed in error).

From there on, the book becomes more of a quick-reference piece for conveyancers, clearly outlining the main areas of interest and potential risk.

This publication is not designed as a comprehensive guide to the legalities of SDLT; there are other (very good) books for that. Rather, it aims to strip out the complexities and focus on what you need to know for everyday practice. It will also highlight areas of more complexity or planning opportunities where additional professional advice may be required.

At the time of writing, the Government had just announced a temporary relief period for residential property purchases in an attempt to stimulate the property market following the coronavirus (Covid-19) pandemic. The relief takes the form of increasing the Nil rate and 3% thresholds to £500,000 and is to be applied from 8 July 2020 to 31 March 2021 inclusive. The changes announced do not affect the application of the SDLT statute book, simply the end calculation.

Relief for first-time buyers is also disapplied during the temporary relief period, instead relief is simply obtained by applying the increased threshold.

All the case studies in this book have applied the normal rates and not the temporary rates.

As you read through each chapter, keep an eye out for these symbols:

Potential risk: An area in which care should be taken	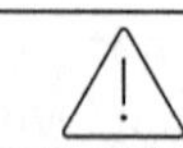
Planning opportunities: A potential opportunity to mitigate the tax exposure	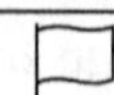

Contents

Chapter One
Introduction

SDLT was introduced in 2003, replacing Stamp Duty for land transactions. For many of the years that followed, the standard 'slab system' applied with the only concerns for those calculating the SDLT charge being the value and nature of the property.

However, over the years HMRC has introduced a raft of new legislation.

A brief history of SDLT	
1 December 2003	SDLT introduced in respect of land transactions
6 December 2006	S75A FA 2003 was introduced (SDLT general anti-avoidance provision) to enable HMRC to combat tax avoidance schemes using legislation instead of litigation (as previously was the case)
19 July 2011	Multiple Dwellings Relief introduced
21 March 2012	15% rate introduced for high value transactions by non-natural persons (threshold £2,000,000)
20 March 2014	15% rate: threshold reduced to £500,000
4 December 2014	'Slice[1]' basis of taxation replaced 'slab[2]' basis for residential property
1 April 2015	Tax raising powers devolved to Scotland: Land and Building Transaction Tax introduced
17 March 2016	'Slice' basis of taxation replaced 'slab' basis for non-residential property
1 April 2016	3% higher rates for additional dwellings and dwellings purchased by companies introduced
22 November 2017	Relief for first-time buyers introduced
1 April 2018	Tax raising powers devolved to Wales: Land Transaction Tax introduced
8 July 2020 – 31 March 2021	Temporary increase to SDLT Nil rate and 3% band for residential properties following the coronavirus (Covid-19) pandemic.
1 April 2021	Proposed introduction of a 2% SDLT surcharge on non-UK residents purchasing residential property in England and Northern Ireland.

The SDLT statute book is now more complex than ever. Accordingly, it is becoming increasingly difficult to remain compliant with the ever-changing rules.

---

[1] Rates applied to the portion of the property value which falls within each band.

[2] Calculated according to which band the total price of the property fell into.

The SDLT charging provisions are contained in Part 4 of Finance Act 2003 (S42 – 124 and Schedules 2A – 19) and as hinted above, are rather complex. However, it is important to take a systematic approach when working through the legislation to ensure its correct application in respect of a specific land transaction. The legislation should be the primary focus.

Case law can be referred to, to assist with the application of the rules.

HMRC's internal guidance manual can be helpful, but it is important to stress that this guidance is HMRC's view of the interpretation of the legislation and not the actual legislation. In some cases, this can give rise to discrepancies and therefore should not be solely relied upon without confirming the legislative basis.

SDLT Rates

The rates at which SDLT is charged is dependent on the nature of the property and type of transaction.

Table A – Entirely Residential Property Transactions

Relevant Consideration	Standard Rate	Higher Rate for Additional Dwellings
Up to £125,000	0%	3%
£125,001 - £250,000	2%	5%
£250,001 - £925,000	5%	8%
£925,001 - £1,500,000	10%	13%
£1,500,001 +	12%	15%

First Time Buyers – Entirely Residential Property Transactions

Relevant Consideration	Rate
Up to £300,000	0%
£300,000 - £500,000	5%
Over £500,000	Standard SDLT rates apply to whole purchase price

Higher Rate for Acquisitions of Residential Property by Certain Non-Natural Persons

Relevant Consideration	Rate
Individual dwelling over £500,000	15%

Residential Leases

Premiums paid for the grant or assignment of a lease are taxed in accordance with Table A (entirely residential) in the normal way.

NPV of rents	Rate
Up to £125,000	0%
£125,001 +	1%

Temporary increase to SDLT Nil rate and 3% band for residential properties following the coronavirus (Covid-19) pandemic

The Nil rate and 3% rate threshold are increased for residential properties purchased from 8 July 2020 until 31 March 2021 (temporary relief period).

Table A – Entirely Residential Property Transactions

Relevant Consideration	Standard Rate	Higher Rate for Additional Dwellings
Up to **£500,000**	0%	3%
£500,001 - £925,000	5%	8%
£925,001 - £1,500,000	10%	13%
£1,500,001 +	12%	15%

Relief for First-Time Buyers

The provisions applicable to first time buyers in section 57B and Schedule 6ZA will be disapplied during the temporary relief period.

Residential Leases

Premiums paid for the grant or assignment of a lease are taxed in accordance with Table A (entirely residential) in the normal way.

NPV of rents	Rate
Up to **£500,000**	0%
£500,001 +	1%

Table B – Non-Residential & Mixed-Use Property Transactions

Relevant consideration	SDLT rate
Up to £150,000	0%
£150,001 - £250,000	2%
£250,001 +	5%

Non-Residential Leases

Premiums paid for the grant or assignment of a lease are taxed in accordance with Table B (non-residential) in the normal way.

Relevant consideration	SDLT rate
Up to £150,000	0%
£150,001 - £5,000,000	1%
£5,000,000 +	2%

Chapter Two
Charging Provisions

At a Glance

SDLT applies to all chargeable **'land transactions'** in England and Northern Ireland.

A land transaction is any **'acquisition'** of a **'chargeable interest'.**

Generally, the **'effective date'** of a land transaction is completion.

The effective date is important as it determines when

- liability to SDLT arises
- the reporting obligations arise
- the conditions for any available relief must be met

The effective date is modified when a contract is substantially performed prior to completion.

Introduction

SDLT applies to all chargeable land transactions in England and Northern Ireland. This chapter provides an overview of the SDLT charge, taking the reader step-by-step through **what SDLT is chargeable on** and **when it is chargeable**. It is important to take a systematic approach and work through the early provisions in the legislation first; this will ensure that land transactions that are within the scope of SDLT are correctly identified and reported (and, by the same token, that land transactions which fall outside the scope are not reported and taxed in error).

The Tax

SDLT was introduced in the UK from 1 December 2003. However, SDLT no longer applies to land transactions in Scotland (since April 2015) or Wales (since April 2018).

The SDLT charging provisions are contained in Part 4 of Finance Act (FA) 2003 (S42 – 124 and Schedules 2A – 19).

S42 FA 2003 introduces the tax known as SDLT, and provides that it is charged on land transactions and is chargeable:

whether or not there is any instrument effecting the transaction	✓
if there is such an instrument, whether or not it is executed in the United Kingdom	✓
whether or not any party to the transaction is present, or resident, in the United Kingdom	✓

Land Transactions

A land transaction[3] is defined as any **acquisition** of a **chargeable interest** and applies however the acquisition is effected:

whether by act of the parties	✓
by order of a court or other authority	✓
by or under any statutory provision, *or*	✓
by operation of law	✓

Acquisition

The legislation details four specific instances when an acquisition of a chargeable interest will occur:

Creation of a chargeable interest is: • an acquisition by the person becoming entitled to the interest created, *and* • a disposal by the person whose interest or right is subject to the interest created.	✓
Surrender or release of a chargeable interest is: • an acquisition of that interest by any person whose interest or right is benefitted or enlarged by the transaction, *and* • a disposal by the person ceasing to be entitled to that interest.	✓
Variation (other than a lease) of a chargeable interest is: • an acquisition of a chargeable interest by the person benefitting from the variation, *and* • a disposal of a chargeable interest by the person whose interest is subject to or limited by the variation.	✓

[3] S43 FA 2003

Variation of a lease is an acquisition and disposal of a chargeable interest only where: • it takes effect, or is treated as taking effect, as the grant of a new lease, *or* • it is varied to reduce the amount of rent or the term of the lease	✓

A 'purchaser' is the person acquiring the subject-matter of the transaction, and the 'vendor' is the person disposing of that interest.

However, a person will not be treated as a purchaser unless he has given consideration for, or is party to, the land transaction.

The purchaser is the person who is required to file a land transaction return and pay any tax due.

Chargeable interest

S48 FA 2003 provides the definition of a **chargeable interest,** being:

An estate, interest, right or power in or over land in England or Northern Ireland,	✓
the benefit of an obligation, restriction or condition affecting the value of any such estate, interest, right or power	✓
other than an **exempt interest**	✗

The HMRC manual[4] provides the following examples of **chargeable interests**:

HMRC examples of chargeable interests	
A freehold estate	✓
A leasehold estate	✓
An undivided share in land	✓
A right in or over land such as an easement or profit a prendre, for example a right of light	✓
A rent-charge	✓
In Northern Ireland, a ground rent or fee farm rent	✓
The right to receive rent	✓
The benefit of a restrictive covenant	✓
The benefit of a positive covenant	✓
An equitable or beneficial interest in land such as a life interest or an interest in reversion or in remainder	✓
An executor's or trustee's power of appointment	✓

[4] SDLTM00280

The legislation provides for the following **exempt** interests[5]:

Exempt interests	
Any security interest (an interests or right [other than a rent-charge] held for the purpose of securing the payment of money or the performance of any other obligation)	✕
A licence to use or occupy land	✕
A tenancy at will	✕
An advowson, franchise (a grant from the Crown such as the right to hold a market or fair, or the right to take tolls) or manor	✕

S48A FA 2003 sets out the rules when a transaction involves land which is partly in England and partly in Wales and provides that it should be treated as two separate land transactions applying a just and reasonable apportionment.

Effective Date

The effective date of a transaction is an important concept as it determines when liability to SDLT arises and when the reporting obligations arise. It is also the date on which the conditions for any available relief must be met.

The general rule is that, except as otherwise provided, the effective date of a land transaction is when that land transaction is completed[6].

However, there are some **exceptions**:

Exceptions to the general rule	
Contract substantially performed prior to completion[7]	✕
Contract providing for conveyance to third party[8]	✕
Contract providing for conveyance to third party and subsequent assignment of rights[9]	✕
Options and rights of pre-emption[10]	✕
Pre-completion transactions[11]	✕
Leases that continue after a fixed term[12]	✕
Agreement for lease followed by substantial performance[13]	✕

[5] S48 (2) FA 2003
[6] S119 FA 2003
[7] S44(4) FA 2003
[8] S44A(3) FA 2003
[9] S45A(8) FA 2003
[10] S46(3) FA 2003
[11] Para 5 Schedule 2A FA 2003
[12] Para 3(4) Schedule 17A FA 2003
[13] Para 12A(2) Schedule 17A FA 2003

Assignment of agreement for lease occurring after agreement substantially performed[14]	✗

The most common exception seen in practice is where the contract is substantially performed before completion.

Contract Substantially Performed Prior to Completion

A contract for a land transaction that contemplates completion by conveyance of the legal estate will have an 'effective date' for SDLT, the earlier of

- 'substantial performance' of the contract or
- the conveyance[15]

The mere entry into a contract itself is ignored and is not regarded as entering into a land transaction[16].

Substantial performance occurs when either:

the purchaser (or a person connected with the purchaser) takes possession of the whole or substantially the whole of the chargeable interest; *or*	✓
a substantial amount of the consideration is paid or provided	✓

A contract for the sale of land will not by itself give rise to a land transaction. In practical terms, further steps to action the contract either by taking possession, paying a substantial amount of the consideration or the eventual conveyance will be required in order to give rise to a land transaction.

The legislation provides that it is immaterial whether the purchaser takes possession under the contract or under a licence or lease of a temporary character[17]. Possession includes receipt of rents and profits or the right to receive them[18].

[14] Para 12B(3) Schedule 17A FA 2003
[15] S44 FA 2003
[16] S44 (2) FA 2003
[17] S44 (6) (b) FA 2003
[18] S44 (6) (a) FA 2003

A **substantial amount** of the consideration is paid or provided:

if none of the consideration is rent, where the whole or substantially the whole of the consideration is paid or provided	✓
if the only consideration is rent, when the first payment of rent is made	✓
if the consideration includes both rent and other consideration, when: • the whole or substantially the whole of the consideration other than rent is paid or provided, *or* • the first payment of rent is made.	✓
HMRC view: A 'substantial amount' of the consideration is taken by HMRC to be an amount that is equal to or greater than 90% of the consideration payable.[19]	✓

If the contract is substantially performed before completion and there is a subsequent conveyance, both the contract and the conveyance are notifiable transactions[20] and additional SDLT is payable on the conveyance to the extent that the SDLT on the conveyance exceeds the SDLT on the contract.

[19] SDLTM07950

[20] S44 (8) FA 2003

Chapter Three
Chargeable Transactions

At a Glance

A land transaction will be chargeable unless it is **exempt.**

Exempt transactions are

- A transaction for no chargeable consideration
- Grant of leases by registered social landlords
- Transfers between spouses on separation or divorce
- Assents and appropriations by personal representatives
- Transfers in connection with the dissolution of civil partnerships
- Variation of testamentary dispositions

Introduction

Once it has been determined that a land transaction has been effected, it must then be ascertained whether it is chargeable. A land transaction will be chargeable unless it is exempt[21]. Schedule 3 FA 2003 details the specific exempted transactions. Where an exemption applies, the transaction will not be notifiable to HMRC. In this chapter, we consider these exemptions and what to watch out for in practice.

Exempt transactions

No chargeable consideration

A land transaction is exempt from charge if there is no chargeable consideration for the transaction. However, there are a number of specific circumstances in which this general rule is overridden, the most notable being:

[21] S49 FA 2003

where the purchaser is a connected company[22]	✗
exchanges & partitions	✗
release, surrender or assumption of debt	✗
certain partnership transactions	✗

See chapters four and 14 for further discussion of these overrides.

Grant of certain leases by registered social landlords

The grant of a lease of a dwelling is exempt from charge if the lease:

is granted by a relevant housing provider to one or more individuals in accordance with certain provisions, and	✓
is for an indefinite term or is terminable by notice of a month or less	✓

Transactions in connection with divorce etc.

A transaction between one party to a marriage and the other is exempt from charge if it is effected:

in pursuance of an order of a court made on granting in respect of the parties a decree of divorce, nullity of marriage or judicial separation	✓
in pursuance of an order of a court made in connection with the dissolution or annulment of the marriage, or the parties' judicial separation, at any time after the granting of such a decree	✓
in pursuance of • an order of a court made at any time under section 22A, 23A or 24A of the Matrimonial Causes Act 1973 (c 18), *or* • an incidental order of a court made under section 8(2) of the Family Law (Scotland) Act 1985 (c 37) by virtue of section 14(1) of that Act.	✓
at any time in pursuance of an agreement of the parties made in contemplation or otherwise in connection with the dissolution or annulment of the marriage, their judicial separation or the making of a separation order in respect of them.	✓

The last provision makes it clear that a land transaction does not have to be effected by way of a court order for it to be exempt from SDLT.

However, it may be prudent that any agreement made in contemplation of the divorce, for instance, is documented in writing and retained on file as evidence of the agreement between the parties, in the event of any future HMRC enquiry.

---

[22] S53 FA 2003

Example:

Adam and Bethany are currently divorcing. It is proposed that Adam will transfer his interest in the former matrimonial home to Bethany. A sealed court order has yet to be obtained but is in the process of being applied for.

Adam has found a new property and would like to exchange prior to the sealed court order being obtained. In order to mitigate Adam's exposure to the 3% higher rates of SDLT on the new purchase, he will need to divest of his interest in the former matrimonial home prior to completion. Bethany is agreeable to this course of action.

Result:

As there is an agreement by the parties which is made in contemplation of their divorce, the transaction is exempt from SDLT. It is advisable that the agreement is documented in writing.

Assents and appropriations by personal representatives

The acquisition of property by a person in or towards satisfaction of his entitlement under or in relation to the will of a deceased person, or on the intestacy of a deceased person, is exempt from charge.

The exemption does not apply if the person acquiring the property gives any consideration for it, other than the assumption of secured debt.

Example:

Under the terms of Clara's Will, the free estate (including a property) is to be distributed equally amongst the beneficiaries, Derek, Edith and Georgia. The executors intend to distribute the property to Derek and Edith and the residual cash to Georgia. No other chargeable consideration will be given on the distribution of the property.

Result:

The distribution of the property to two of the beneficiaries, in satisfaction of their entitlement under the terms of the Will, will be an exempt land transaction for the purposes of SDLT.

Transactions in connection with the dissolution of civil partnerships

A transaction between one party to a civil partnership and the other is exempt from charge if it is effected:

In pursuance of an order of a court made on granting in respect of the parties an order or decree for the dissolution or annulment of the civil partnership or their judicial separation.	✓
in pursuance of an order of a court made in connection with the dissolution or annulment of the civil partnership, or the parties' judicial separation, at any time after the granting of such an order or decree for dissolution, annulment or judicial separation as mentioned above.	✓
in pursuance of— • an order of a court made at any time under any provision of Schedule 5 to the Civil Partnership Act 2004 that corresponds to section 22A, 23A or 24A of the Matrimonial Causes Act 1973, *or* • an incidental order of a court made under any provision of the Civil Partnership Act 2004 that corresponds to section 8(2) of the Family Law (Scotland) Act 1985 by virtue of section 14(1) of that Act of 1985.	✓
at any time in pursuance of an agreement of the parties made in contemplation of or otherwise in connection with the dissolution or annulment of the civil partnership, their judicial separation or the making of a separation order in respect of them.	✓

Again, it is suggested that any agreement made in contemplation of the dissolution of the civil partnership is documented in writing and retained on file as evidence of the agreement between the parties, in the event of any future HMRC enquiry.

Variation of testamentary dispositions etc

A transaction following a person's death that varies a disposition (whether effected by will, under the law relating to intestacy or otherwise) of property of which the deceased was competent to dispose is exempt from charge **if** the following conditions are met:

That the transaction is carried out within the period of two years after a person's death, *and*	✓
That no consideration in money or money's worth other than the making of a variation of another such disposition is given for it.	✓

The exemption applies whether or not the administration of the estate is complete or the property has been distributed in accordance with the original dispositions.

Example:

Habib is the sole beneficiary of Ibriz's Will, under which Habib has inherited an investment property.

Following taking third party tax advice, Habib is considering transferring the property into a limited company for income tax mitigation purposes.

Result:

The transfer of the property to a company will be exempt if it is effected by way of a Deed of Variation made within 2 years of the date of Ibriz's death and provided no chargeable consideration is given (except the assumption of secured debt).

Chapter Four
Chargeable Consideration

At a Glance

SDLT is payable on the chargeable consideration paid in respect of the land transaction.

Schedule 4 FA 2003 details the rules for determining the chargeable consideration of the land transaction, the most notable being:

- Money or money's worth
- Debt as consideration
- Transfer of other property (exchanges and partitions)
- Carrying out of works

There are special rules in relation to contingent, uncertain or unascertained consideration.

The chargeable consideration is deemed to be the market value where the purchaser is a connected company.

Introduction

Once it has been determined that a land transaction is chargeable, the question then arises as to **what amount is chargeable**. Schedule 4 FA 2003 makes provision as to the chargeable consideration for a land transaction.

It is important to correctly identify the quantum of the chargeable consideration to ensure the correct amount of SDLT is assessed and reported. Let's look at some different situations, and how circumstances can affect how we calculate chargeable consideration.

Chargeable consideration

The chargeable consideration for a transaction is, except as otherwise expressly provided, any consideration in money or money's worth given for the subject-matter of the transaction, directly or indirectly, by the purchaser or a person connected with him[23].

Therefore, in most typical scenarios, SDLT is payable on the amount of money exchanged in the land transaction.

[23] Paragraph 1 Schedule 4 FA 2003

However, Schedule 4 FA 2003 provides for further circumstances in which chargeable consideration can arise.

Debt as consideration

Paragraph 8 of Schedule 4 provides the following circumstances in which debt can represent chargeable consideration:

The satisfaction of debt due to the purchaser or owed by the vendor	✓
The release of debt due to the purchaser or owed by the vendor	✓
The assumption of existing debt by the purchaser	✓

The amount of debt satisfied, released or assumed shall be taken to be the whole or, as the case may be, part of the chargeable consideration for the transaction.

In practice, this is most typically seen where property is gifted, and the 'purchaser' becomes responsible for the whole or a proportion of the existing mortgage.

Example:

James wishes to gift an investment property worth £300,000 to Kurt, as part of his wider inheritance tax planning. The remaining mortgage on the property is £175,000.

From an SDLT perspective, although the transfer is a gift with no money exchanging hands, Kurt will take on the entire mortgage. Accordingly, the chargeable consideration of the land transaction is £175,000.

Consideration of the other tax implications associated with the gift is required.

From an inheritance tax perspective, the gift will be treated as a Potentially Exempt Transfer (PET) and the value of the property will fall entirely outside James' estate if he survives 7 years.

From a capital gains tax perspective, the gift will be deemed to occur at market value and therefore a 'dry tax' charge will arise on the uplift in value from the acquisition date.

Therefore, James' inheritance tax planning will give rise to both an upfront SDLT and CGT tax charge.

Exchanges

Where a land transaction is entered into by the purchaser (alone or jointly) wholly or partly in consideration of another land transaction being entered into by him (alone or jointly) as vendor:

- each transaction is taxed as if it were distinct and separate from the other; *and*

- special rules determine the chargeable consideration[24].

A land transaction is treated as an exchange in any case where an obligation to give consideration for a land transaction that a person enters into as purchaser is met wholly or partly by way of that person entering into another transaction as vendor:[25]

The amount of the chargeable consideration will depend on whether the subject matter of any of the transactions is a major interest in land[26].

In the case of an exchange, the general charging provision (money or money's worth) is overruled so that the transactions are treated as separate land transactions occurring at:

- the higher of the market value of the chargeable interest acquired *and*
- the value or amount of the consideration given[27].

Care is required where the properties to be exchanged are of unequal value. In such cases, HMRC accept that the consideration given may need to be apportioned to determine the chargeable consideration given for the interest received. This apportionment has to be on a just and reasonable basis[28].	⚠

If the more expensive interest is given partly in consideration for another interest and partly in respect of another matter (for example, making a gift or for the receipt of cash) then its value should be apportioned between the chargeable consideration for the interest acquired and the other matter.

HMRC consider that there is unlikely to be any element of gift in any transaction which has a commercial flavour.

[24] S47 (1) FA 2003
[25] S47 (2) FA 2003
[26] Paragraph 5 (3) Schedule 4 FA 2003
[27] Paragraph 5 Schedule 4 FA 2003
[28] Para 4 Schedule 4 FA 2003

Example:

Lars owns a property worth £500,000 and Maha owns another property valued at £300,000.

On an exchange of the properties, Maha would be subject to SDLT on £500,000 (the market value of the interest acquired - this is greater than the consideration she gave i.e. the value of property being £300,000).

Lars must pay SDLT on the greater of the market value of the interest acquired (£300,000) and the chargeable consideration given (£500,000).

HMRC accept that a just and reasonable apportionment results in the chargeable consideration given being £300,000 and a gift of £200,000.

Result:

Lars pays SDLT on £300,000 and Maha pays SDLT on £500,000.

Partitions

In the case of a partition of a chargeable interest to which persons are jointly entitled, the share of the interest held by the purchaser immediately before the partition does not count as chargeable consideration.[29]

Accordingly, where land is held jointly, the rules discussed above in relation to exchanges are disapplied[30]. For these purposes, 'jointly entitled' means beneficially entitled as joint tenants or tenants in common.

Therefore, if the parties are splitting the properties so they each hold properties of the same value, there would be no chargeable consideration and therefore no SDLT payable.

This position is confirmed in HMRC manual SDLTM34110, which provides:

> *Where a partnership is not involved, if A & B each own 50% of two properties and decide to take one specific property each, the exchange rules are overridden by FA03/Sch4/para5(6) and are to be replaced by the rules under FA03/Sch4/para6 ('partition'). A charge will only be made on a partition if equality money is to be paid between the parties.*

---

[29] Paragraph 6 Schedule 4 FA 2003

[30] Paragraph 5 (6) Schedule 4 FA 2003

Care is required if an equalisation payment is made or debt is assumed as part of the partition. In such circumstances, SDLT will be chargeable on these separate amounts. Separate rules apply for cases involving partnership partitions (see chapter 15).	⚠

Example:

Nick and Olivia hold four rental properties in joint names. Two of the properties are worth £150,000 and two are worth £200,000. There are no mortgages on any of the properties.

After the partition, Nick will hold the entirety of one property valued at £150,000 and one at £200,000. Olivia will hold the entirety of the other two properties.

Under the special partition rules, the interests exchanged will not count as chargeable consideration. Accordingly, as no other money or interests are exchanged, no SDLT payable will be payable in respect to this transaction.

If on the other hand, as part of the partition it is agreed that Nick will hold the entirety of both properties valued at £150,000 and Olivia takes the interest in the more expensive properties but in addition, Olivia will make an equalisation payment of £50,000.

SDLT will be payable on £50,000.

Similarly, a charge to SDLT may arise if, on the partition, one party assumes the entire mortgage on the property being partitioned.

Carrying out of works

Where the whole or part of the consideration of a land transaction involves the purchaser carrying out construction work (including improvement or repair of a building, or other works to enhance the value of the land), the value of the works can count as chargeable consideration.

Paragraph 10 of Schedule 4 provides the rules for determining whether the costs of carrying out works should be chargeable.

If the costs meet ALL the specified conditions below, the value of the works does not count as chargeable consideration. In all other cases, the value of the works should be taken in account as chargeable consideration.

The specified conditions are that:

the works are carried out after the effective date of the transaction	✓
the works are carried out on land acquired or to be acquired under the transaction or on other land held by the purchaser or a person connected with him	✓
it is not a condition of the transaction that the works are carried out by the vendor or a person connected with him.	✓

Where the value of building works is included in the chargeable consideration the value is taken to be the amount that would have to be paid in the open market for the carrying out of the works in question.

Example:

Prefab Ltd, a construction company, enters into a contract to acquire a plot of land from Quantum Ltd.

Under the terms of the contract, Prefab Ltd is to pay £1,000,000 for the land and, in addition, Prefab Ltd is required to build a new workshop for Quantum Ltd on another plot of land owned by Quantum Ltd.
The cost of the construction of the new workshop is estimated to be £750,000.

The chargeable consideration in this case is £1,750,000.

Example:

Ross Ltd, a construction company, enters into a contract to acquire a plot of land from Standard Fittings Ltd.

Under the terms of the contract, Ross Ltd is to pay £1,000,000 for the land and in addition, Ross Ltd must construct a workshop for Standard Fittings Ltd on the purchased land after completion. The value of the works is £750,000.

The chargeable consideration in this case is £1,000,000.

Contingent, Uncertain or Unascertained Consideration

Contingent consideration

Where the whole or part of the chargeable consideration for a transaction is contingent, the amount or value of the consideration shall be determined on the assumption that the outcome of the contingency will be such that the consideration is payable or, as the case may be, does not cease to be payable.

Uncertain or Unascertainable consideration

Where the whole or part of the chargeable consideration for a transaction is uncertain or unascertained, its amount or value shall be determined using a reasonable estimate.

'Contingent' is defined as:

that it is to be paid or provided only if some uncertain future event occurs, *or*	✓
that it is to cease to be paid or provided if some uncertain future event occurs.	✓

'Uncertain' means that its amount or value depends on uncertain future events.

An adjustment is required once the contingency occurs (or it becomes clear that it will not occur) or in the case of uncertain or unascertained consideration, whenever any relevant amount becomes ascertained[31].

A claim for **deferral** can be made in respect of **contingent or uncertain consideration**, where the consideration is payable more than **six months** after the effective date of the transaction[32].

A **deferral** is **not available** in respect of **unascertainable** consideration.

The S53 Trap – Connected Companies

S53 FA 2003 provides that when a company purchases a chargeable interest and the vendor is connected[33] with the company or some or all of the consideration consists of the issue or transfer of shares in any company with which the vendor is connected, the chargeable consideration is to be taken to be:

not less than the market value of the interest acquired at the effective date of the transaction, *plus*	✓
any rent if the acquisition is the grant of a lease	✓

• The fact that there may be no chargeable consideration actually given for the transfer does not affect the application of the market value rule.	⚠

[31] S80 FA 2003

[32] S90 FA 2003

[33] S1122 CTA 2010 provides the definition of 'connected' for these purposes

• However, any other available exemption or relief from SDLT overrides the market value rule[34].	

There are three **specific exceptions** to the market value rule contained at S54 FA 2003.

Specific exemptions	
Case 1	Immediately after the transaction, the company holds the property as trustee in the course of a business carried on by it that consists of (or includes) the management of trusts.
Case 2	– Immediately after the transaction the company holds the property as trustee, *and* – the vendor is connected with the company only because of S 1122(6) CTA 2010 (connection by virtue of acting in the capacity as trustee of a settlement)
Case 3	– The vendor is a company and the transaction is, or is part of, a distribution of the assets of that company (whether or not in connection with its winding up), *and* – it is not the case that i. the subject-matter of the transaction, or ii. an interest from which that interest is derived, has, within the period of three years immediately preceding the effective date of the transaction, been the subject of a transaction in respect of which group relief was claimed by the vendor.

Practical implications

It does not matter how the transfer of the property to the company is structured.

Market value rule applies regardless if	
The property is gifted for no consideration	✕
The property is transferred along with a sole trade business in exchange for shares	✕
The property is sold at undervalue for cash	✕

The company's SDLT charge will be calculated by reference to the market value of the property.

[34] S53(4) FA 2003

If a commercial or mixed-use property is transferred, the rates at Table B will be applied. Residential properties will be taxed using the rates at Table A.

However, planning may be available where there is a transfer of multiple dwellings.

If six or more dwellings are being transferred, the properties are treated as non-residential property and therefore the lower rates contained at Table B can be applied	
Where two or more dwellings are transferred, consider claiming Multiple Dwellings Relief (see chapter twelve)	
There may be other tax implications associated with the transfer of properties to a company, most notably, CGT. These should be considered in full prior to any transfers.	

Example:

Toni owns 12 residential properties as investment properties with a total value of £1,615,000. As a result of the interest restriction rules, Toni would like to transfer the properties to a limited company (which she will hold 100% of the shares in) for no consideration.

By virtue of S53 FA 2003, SDLT will be payable on the total aggregated market value (as linked transaction) of the properties of £1,615,000, which gives rise to SDLT of £156,000 (applying the rates at Table A with the 3% surcharge).

However, as 6 or more properties are being transferred, the rates at Table B can be applied to give SDLT payable of £70,250.

Moreover, instead of applying the rates at Table B, a claim for MDR can be made with the resultant SDLT of £50,748

The HMRC SDLT Calculator will not pick up the non-residential rate for six or more dwellings or the availability of MDR.

Partnership incorporations

As noted above, the transfer of a property on the incorporation of a sole trade will give rise to an SDLT charge based on the market value of the property. However, there are special rules for certain transactions involving partnerships which take priority over S53 FA 2003, so that S53 does not apply in respect of partnership incorporations.

Instead, the provisions contained at Para 18 of Schedule 15 will apply to calculate the chargeable consideration. In some cases involving partnership incorporations, the chargeable consideration can be reduced to Nil. This is discussed in further detail at chapter 15.

The rules are complex, and care should be exercised when carrying out the calculation.	⚠

For instance, there is a grey area in relation to the incorporation of a partnership with a property portfolio and whether this consists of a 'business' or the mere passive holding of investments. The requirement of a business being necessary to fall within the special partnership provisions.

Reference can be made to the case of *Elizabeth Moyne Ramsay v HMRC TC 1871 for* consideration of what constitutes a business in these circumstances.

Again, this is a complex area, and specialist advice should be sought in cases of doubt.

Example:

The same facts as in the above example, except that the properties are held as partnership assets by a partnership consisting of Toni & Ursula, as opposed to Toni holding them in her sole name (as above). Both partners actively manage the property portfolio and would like to transfer the properties to a limited company in which they will each hold 50% of the shares in the new company.

In this case, by applying the special formula[35]:

MV x (SLP – 100)%, the SLP is calculated as 100.

Therefore, the chargeable consideration is Nil as the multiplier in this case will be zero.

[35] Para 18 Schedule 15 FA 2003

Chapter Five
Amount of Tax Chargeable

At a Glance

SDLT is charged at different rates depending on the type of property.

Table A: relevant land consists entirely of residential property.

Table B: relevant land is not residential or mixed-use.

Interpretive issues as key terms are not defined in the legislation.

However, practitioners now have more clarity as a result of:

- Updated HMRC manual guidance (SDLTM00360 – SDLTM00480).
- Several First Tier Tribunal decisions.

The purchase of six or more dwellings is classified as non-residential property.

The legislation lists other buildings which are specifically to be treated as non-residential property, including halls of residence for students, hotels and care homes.

Introduction

Once the quantum of chargeable consideration has been confirmed, it then turns to establish which rates of tax are to be applied. The rate applied is dependent on whether the property is residential or non-residential in nature. In this chapter, we're going to look at what constitutes residential and non-residential property, including some recent case law rulings on grey areas.

Rate of SDLT applicable

Table A – Residential Property Rates

S55 FA 2003 provides for the amount of tax chargeable in respect of land transactions and directs that where the 'relevant land' consists entirely of residential property, the rates at Table A (read in conjunction with Schedule 4ZA Pt 1 FA 2003) should be applied.

Relevant consideration	SDLT rate	Higher SDLT rate for additional dwellings
Up to £125,000	0%	3%
£125,001 - £250,000	2%	5%
£250,001 - £925,000	5%	8%
£925,001 - £1,500,000	10%	13%
£1,500,001 +	12%	15%

For transactions completed (or substantially performed) between 8 July 2020 and 31 March inclusive, the following rates should be applied:

Relevant Consideration	Standard Rate	Higher Rate for Additional Dwellings
Up to £500,000	0%	3%
£500,001 - £925,000	5%	8%
£925,001 - £1,500,000	10%	13%
£1,500,001 +	12%	15%

Certain acquisitions of additional dwellings and dwellings by companies will be subject to an additional 3% surcharge applied to the standard rates[36] (see chapters six to eight).

Furthermore, the above rates do not apply to the following:

Acquisitions of residential property by non-natural persons to which the 15% rate applies[37] (see chapter nine)	✕
The exercise of collective rights by tenants of flats[38]	✕

The rate is applied on a banding system, with SDLT calculated on the portion of the chargeable consideration falling within each band. This regime replaced the old 'slab system', which calculated SDLT at a flat rate according to which band the total chargeable consideration of the property fell into.

The banding system of calculating SDLT has applied for residential property from 4 December 2014 and 17 March 2016 for non-residential or mixed-use transactions.

[36] Schedule 4ZA FA 2003

[37] Schedule 4A FA 2003

[38] S74 1A) FA 2003

Example:

The SDLT on a land transaction consisting of entirely residential property (not applying the 3% surcharge) with chargeable consideration of £650,000 would be calculated as follows:

Relevant consideration (£)	SDLT rate	SDLT (£)
125,000	0%	0
125,000	2%	2,500
400,000	5%	20,000
650,000		**22,500**

Table B – Non-Residential Property

If the relevant land consists of or includes land that is not entirely residential property, then the rates at Table B should be applied.

Relevant consideration	SDLT rate
Up to £150,000	0%
£150,001 - £250,000	2%
£250,001 +	5%

Interaction with Linked Transaction Provisions

Per S55 (4) FA 2003, the 'relevant land' refers to the subject-matter of the transaction and any transactions with which it is linked.

Therefore, the acquisition of residential property is taxed in accordance with the (lower) rates in Table B if it is linked with the acquisition of another transaction that does not refer exclusively to residential property. See chapter 16 for further discussion on 'linked transactions'.

This is confirmed at HMRC guidance SDLTM00360, which states:

> *It follows from s55(1C) that where linked transactions contain a mixture of residential and non-residential land the non-residential rates will be applicable to each of the linked transactions. There is no apportionment of residential/non-residential rates.*

Example:

A father and daughter are purchasing a house and agricultural land from a local farmer, in separate transactions. The father is purchasing the house in bare trust for his daughter but will retain the beneficial interest of the agricultural land. The house will be the daughter's main residence and the father will continue to farm the agricultural land. The transactions will be documented under two separate contracts.

Parents and children are connected for the purposes of S1122 CTA 2010.

As the two transactions are between the same vendor and connected purchasers, they will fall within the linked transactions provisions. Accordingly, as the property in both linked transactions does not consist entirely of residential property, the rates at Table B should be applied.

This can be especially tax efficient, where the residential property would attract the 3% higher rates of SDLT.

Meaning of residential property

Given the introduction of the 3% surcharge and 15% rate for certain transactions involving companies (and other non-natural persons), the distinction between residential and non-residential property has become more prominent in recent years. HMRC appear to be scrutinising claims of non-residential property in more detail than before.

S116 FA 2003 provides the definition of residential and non-residential property as:

> *In this Part **"residential property"** means—*
>
> *(a) a building that is used or suitable for use as a dwelling, or is in the process of being constructed or adapted for such use, and*
>
> *(b) land that is or forms part of the garden or grounds of a building within paragraph (a) (including any building or structure on such land), or*
>
> *(c) an interest in or right over land that subsists for the benefit of a building within paragraph (a) or of land within paragraph (b);*
>
> *and **"non-residential property"** means any property that is not residential property.*

The important point to note is that Table A only applies if 'the relevant land consists entirely of residential property' and Table B applies 'if the relevant land includes land that is not residential property'.

Therefore, if the whole of the property falls within S116 (1(a), (b) or (c), the rates in Table A would apply, but if any part of the property falls outside those paragraphs (and so is not residential property), the whole of the property is mixed use and the rates at Table B will be applied.

Interpretative issues

Although 'residential property' is defined, the underlying key concepts of 'used or suitable for use', 'dwelling' and 'garden and grounds' are not statutorily defined.

Prior to 2019, taxpayers and practitioners had little guidance as to what constituted these key terms and typically relied upon non-SDLT specific case law, guidance contained in HMRC's Capital Gains Tax manuals in relation to Principal Private Residence relief, HMRC's Statement of Practice 1/04 and general dictionary definitions to substantiate their claim.

However, HMRC made two key updates to their guidance in June and October 2019 providing further guidance on their interpretation of these terms.

Moreover, there have now been a number of specific SDLT cases heard by the First Tier Tribunal dealing with the interpretation of these terms.

Key updates to HMRC manuals

SDLTM00360 – SDLTM00365A (Dated 1 October 2019)	The distinction between **residential and non-residential property**.
SDLTM00380 – SDLTM00400 (Dated 1 October 2019)	What constitutes a **dwelling**, and guidance on the terms **'suitable for use'**, **'mixed use'** and **'in the process of being constructed or adapted for use as a dwelling'.**
SDLTM00410 – SDLTM00430 (Dated 1 October 2019).	Guidance on how to determine the **number of dwellings** forming part of a land transaction. This is helpful when considering – Multiple Dwellings Relief – 3% higher rates involving multiple dwelling purchases – Classification of non-residential property by virtue of consisting of 6 or more dwellings
SDLTM00440 to SDLTM00480 (Dated 25 June 2019)	The meaning of **garden or grounds** for the definition of residential property.

Recent case law

At the time of writing, the only cases on these definitions for SDLT purposes have been heard by the First Tier Tribunal. It should be noted that, whilst they are of persuasive authority, they are not binding.

PN Bewley Ltd (TC6951) – 'Suitable for use as a dwelling'

The case of PN Bewley Ltd v HMRC concerned the purchase of a derelict bungalow and land with planning permission for demolition and building of a new dwelling. The key issue in this case was whether the property was suitable for use as a dwelling at the effective date for the purposes of applying the 3% higher rates of SDLT.

Key points

- The tribunal found in favour of the taxpayer
- Parliament contemplated that there must be a class of buildings that are capable of being a dwelling, but which are unsuitable for that purpose
- Question of fact based on the evidence of the specific case
- Review of other tax law using the exact phrase demonstrates that accidental damage, damage which was not accidental but was caused by events beyond the control of the owner, partial demolition, repairs or any other physical change to the building or its environment could make a building unsuitable for use as a dwelling
- The intention of the purchaser is not relevant. The test is whether it is 'suitable' to be used as a dwelling at the effective date; it is not whether it is capable of becoming so used in the future. Accordingly, the planning permission obtained by the vendor in that case was irrelevant.
- The tribunal considered that the bungalow at the date of completion did not contain what established case law considered the minimum facilities for a building to be a home and therefore a dwelling
- As a result, the tribunal concluded that the 3% higher rates did not apply and therefore the property also de facto failed to be defined as consisting of entirely residential property. Accordingly, it was held to be non-residential property and the rates at Table B were applied.

At Para 53 of the decision the tribunal concluded:

> *"No doubt a passing tramp or group of squatters could have lived in the bungalow as it was at the date of purchase. But taking into account the state of the building as shown in the photographs on Mrs. Bewley's phone with radiators and pipework removed and with the presence of asbestos preventing any repairs or alterations that would not pose a risk to those carrying them out, we have no hesitation in saying that in this case the bungalow was not suitable for use as a dwelling".*

This case provides practical implications when considering:

- if a transaction is entirely residential
- whether there is a dwelling for the purposes of the 3% surcharge or 15% rate
- application of Multiple Dwellings Relief.

Hyman (TC7271) – Garden or Grounds

In the Hyman case, the taxpayer had paid the residential rates (Table A) on their property purchase, but subsequently made an amendment to the SDLT return, claiming a refund on the basis that the property should have been classified as mixed-use, so that the rates at Table B should have been applied.

As well as a farmhouse, the property in question consisted of two gardens, a duck pond, barn, and a meadow with a public bridleway running through it. It was contended that the transaction did not consist entirely of residential property because

- the barn, meadow and bridleway were physically separated from the dwelling by hedges
- the bridleway was used by the public on a daily basis and therefore could not be used by the appellant for private or recreational purposes
- the meadow and barn were not necessary or integral parts of the property and could not be used for ornamental or recreational purposes
- the barn was classified as a non-residential building and the appellant would need planning permission to change the use
- at the time of writing, it is understood that this case is subject to appeal

Key points

- The tribunal found in favour of HMRC and rejected the taxpayer's submissions that the barn, meadow and bridleway did not form part of the 'garden or grounds'
- The Judge held that 'grounds' has, and was intended to have, a wide meaning. The Judge concluded that in its ordinary meaning, 'grounds' means land that is attached to or surrounding a house, which is occupied with the house, and is available to its owners to use.
- It is not a necessary feature of grounds that they are used for ornamental or recreational purposes
- Not relevant if separated by hedges or fences
- Rights of way impinging on owner's enjoyment does make the 'grounds' any less the grounds

- Land would **not** be 'grounds' to the extent that it is used for a separate, say commercial, purpose because it would not then be occupied with the residence, but would be premises on which a business is conducted.

Goodfellow (TC07507) – Mixed-use and Garden and Grounds

This case followed the Hyman decision and involved the same representatives on both sides with the judge adopting much of the reasoning of Hyman.

The SDLT return was submitted on the basis that the land transaction was entirely residential, and a subsequent overpayment claim was made to the effect that the transaction did not consist entirely of residential property because:

- the space above the garage was used as an office for the taxpayer's business; and
- the stable yard and paddocks were used by a third party for grazing horses (rent £1 per month).

Key points

- The tribunal held in favour of HMRC
- The home office was found to be suitable for domestic use and accordingly wholly residential in character
- The paddocks were held to form part of the grounds for recreational purposes and the rental arrangement was deemed to be the modern equivalent of a peppercorn rental

Myles-Till (TC07633) – Garden and Grounds

The case of Myles-Till v HMRC involved the purchase of a house along with a paddock of about 1.1 acres situated behind the rear garden, enclosed by hedging and post and rail fencing. In 1983, the paddock formed part of a neighbouring farm. For many years, up to and including January 2017, the paddock had been covered in grass and therefore potentially usable for pasture i.e. grazing animals. There was no evidence of actual business use since 1983 and the sales particulars said the paddock provided a view for the dwelling.

The case involved an amended SDLT return claiming mixed-use over the previously reported residential rate. In the first instance, HMRC processed the amendment and made a repayment, but later opened an enquiry into the amendment.

Key points

- The Tribunal agreed with HMRC that the property counted as "residential property" because the paddock constituted part of the "grounds" of the dwelling.
- The decision rejected HMRC's argument that it is enough for the land to be owned with the dwelling or to be available for the owners to use as they wish.
- There was clear emphasis on the use or function of the land, and the issue of whether the land supports the use of the building as a dwelling. *For the adjoining land to be "grounds", it must be, functionally, an appendage to the dwelling, rather than having a self-standing function.*
- In the absence of evidence of commercial use of the paddock for many years, the fact that the paddock provided views from the building was held to be enough to make the land an appendage to the dwelling.

Statute Defined Residential Property - Buildings used for Specific Purposes

A building used for any of the following purposes is treated as used as a dwelling and is therefore considered residential property:

Residential accommodation for school pupils	✓
Residential accommodation for students, other than a hall of residence for students in further or higher education	✓
Residential accommodation for members of the armed forces	✓
An institution that is the sole or main residence of at least 90% of its residents and does not fall within any of specified categories of buildings not used as a dwelling (see below)	✓

Statute Defined Non-Residential Property

Where **six or more** separate dwellings are the subject of a single transaction involving the transfer of a major interest in, or the grant of a lease over, them, then, those dwellings are treated **as not being residential property[39].**

The following buildings are not used as a dwelling and are therefore classified as **non-residential[40]**:

[39] S116 (7) FA 2003

[40] S116 (3) FA 2003

A home or other institution providing residential accommodation for children	✗
A hall of residence for students in further or higher education	✗
A home or other institution providing residential accommodation with personal care for persons in need of personal care by reason of old age, disablement, past or present dependence on alcohol or drugs or past or present mental disorder	✗
A hospital or hospice	✗
A prison or similar establishment	✗
A hotel or inn or similar establishment	✗

Chapter Six

3% Higher Rates for Additional Dwellings - SCHEDULE 4ZA FA 2003

At a Glance

There is a 3% higher rate of SDLT on transactions involving the acquisition of additional dwellings.

Different rules apply depending on the number of properties acquired and who acquires them.

Non-residential or mixed-use transactions: 3% does not apply.

Transactions between spouses/civil partners: 3% does not apply.

Joint purchasers: 3% applies if any of the joint purchasers meet the conditions.

Spouses/civil partners acting alone: 3% applies if the other spouse/civil partner (not party to the transaction) meets the conditions.

The legislation treats the acquisition of a single dwelling and the acquisition of multiple dwellings separately and, within each category, deals first with acquisitions by individuals and then acquisitions by purchasers who are not individuals.

Introduction

An additional 3% higher rate of SDLT applies to certain residential property transactions that involve the acquisition of additional dwellings.

In this chapter, we'll identify when the 3% higher rate applies (and when it doesn't).

Background

The provisions contained in Schedule 4ZA FA 2003 were introduced in respect of land transactions from 1 April 2016, subject to transactions effected in pursuance of a contract entered into and substantially performed before 26 November 2015.

The provisions apply an additional 3% surcharge to the rates contained at **Table A** for certain acquisitions of additional properties.

Relevant consideration	Higher SDLT rate
Up to £125,000	3%
£125,001 - £250,000	5%
£250,001 - £925,000	8%
£925,001 - £1,500,000	13%
£1,500,001 +	15%

For transactions completed (or substantially performed) between 8 July 2020 and 31 March inclusive, the following rates should be applied:

Relevant Consideration	Higher SDLT rate
Up to £500,000	3%
£500,001 - £925,000	8%
£925,001 - £1,500,000	13%
£1,500,001 +	15%

When the 3% Higher Rates will Not Apply

Non-residential or mixed-use properties	✕
Transactions where the consideration is less than £40,000	✕
Freehold or leasehold interests with a term of less than 7 years to run on the effective date	✕
Spouses/civil partners purchasing from one another – transactions between one spouse/civil partner and the other (who are living together) are not higher rate transactions	✕
High value residential property transactions where the 15% charge applies. Care required where purchase includes a chargeable interest that is not a higher threshold interest	✕
In most cases, purchases of caravans, houseboats and mobile homes	✕

When the 3% Higher Rates will Apply

Sole purchaser - the transaction will be a higher rates transaction if it falls within the specified conditions relating to single or multiple dwelling purchases[41]	✓
Joint purchasers - the higher rates will apply if the transaction would be a higher rates transaction for any of the purchasers considered individually, i.e. if there are two individual purchasers and the conditions are satisfied for one of them only, the entire transaction will be charged at the higher rates[42] ***Example:*** Valerie and Walter are purchasing a dwelling. Valerie meets the conditions, Walter does not. The transaction will be subject to the 3% higher rates.	✓
Spouses/civil partners purchasing alone - where one spouse/civil partner is purchasing alone, and the other spouse/civil partner meets the conditions for the higher rates, the transaction will be deemed to be a higher rates transaction even if the purchasing spouse/civil partner does not satisfy the conditions. ***Example:*** Xavier is purchasing a property in his sole name. Xavier does not meet the conditions for the 3% higher rates to apply, but his wife, Yolanda, does meet the conditions. The transaction will be subject to the 3% higher rates.	✓

There must be an acquisition of a **major interest** in a single/multiple **dwelling** for the higher rates to apply.

- **Major interest -** an interest in a dwelling is a major interest if it is a freehold or leasehold interest.[43] For these purposes, any term of years absolute or leasehold estate is not a 'major interest' if its term does not exceed 7 years on the date of

[41] Paragraph 2 (2) Schedule 4ZA FA 2003
[42] Paragraph 2 (3) Schedule 4ZA FA 2003
[43] S. 117 FA 2003

its grant[44]. The definition of a major interest in a dwelling was clarified by FA 2019 to include an undivided share in a major interest in a dwelling[45].

- **Dwelling –**

Legislative definition of 'dwelling' for the purposes of the higher rates[46]	
It is used or suitable for use as a single dwelling See *P N Bewley Ltd v Revenue and Customs Commissioners [2019] UKFTT 65 (TC)* for discussion on what constitutes 'suitable for use' as a dwelling for these purposes	✓
It is in the process of being constructed or adapted for such use	✓
Land that is, or is to be, occupied or enjoyed with a dwelling as a garden or grounds (including any building or structure on that land) is taken to be part of that dwelling. However, a transaction of such land without the purchase of the actual dwelling will not be liable to the higher rates.	✓
Off-plan purchases can also count as a dwelling where certain conditions are met[47]	✓
A building or part of a building used for the purposes specified in S116 (2) [which are normally treated as dwellings for SDLT purposes] or (3) FA 2003 [which are not normally treated as dwellings for SDLT purposes] is not used as a dwelling for the purposes of the higher rates.	✓

Detailed HMRC guidance

SDLTM00360 – SDLTM00365A (Dated 1 October 2019)	The distinction between **residential and non-residential property**.
SDLTM00380 – SDLTM00400 (Dated 1 October 2019)	What constitutes a **dwelling**, and guidance on the terms 'suitable for use', 'mixed use' and 'in the process of being constructed or adapted for use as a dwelling'.
SDLTM00410 – SDLTM00430 (Dated 1 October 2019).	Guidance on how to determine the **number of dwellings** forming part of a land transaction.
SDLTM00440 to SDLTM00480 (Dated 25 June 2019)	The meaning of **garden or grounds** for the definition of residential property.

[44] Paragraph 2 (4) Schedule 4ZA FA 2003
[45] Paragraph 2 (5) Schedule 4ZA FA 2003
[46] Paragraph 18 Schedule 4ZA FA 2003
[47] Para 18 (5) Schedule 4ZA FA 2003

Application

Different rules apply depending on the number of properties acquired and who acquires them. The legislation deals with the application of the rules as follows:

- Acquisition of a **single dwelling**
  - acquisitions by individuals
  - acquisitions by purchasers who are not individuals

- Acquisition of **multiple dwellings**
  - acquisitions by individuals
  - acquisitions by purchasers who are not individuals

Chapters 7 and 8 consider these in more detail.

Chapter Seven
3% Higher Rates for Additional Dwellings – Single Dwelling Transactions

At a Glance

There are different rules for the acquisition of a single property, depending on whether the purchaser is an individual or not.

For individuals, four conditions must be met in order for the 3% higher rates to apply.

For companies, two conditions must be met in order for the 3% rates to apply.

For trustees, it depends on the type of trust.

A refund of the additional 3% paid may be available where a previous main residence is disposed of within 3 years of purchasing a main residence.

Introduction

The legislation sets out two sets of conditions (for individuals and companies, respectively) that must be met for the 3% higher SDLT rate to apply. The first two conditions are s are straightforward, but the last two conditions require a closer look. In this chapter, we'll look at these conditions and the practical implications associated with determining whether or not they apply.

Individuals

Background

A transaction involving the acquisition of a single dwelling by an individual will be a higher-rate transaction if ALL Conditions A to D are met. [48] If any of Conditions A – D are not met, then the higher rates will not apply to the purchase.

Accordingly, each condition should be considered in turn and if a condition is not satisfied, there is no need to examine the remaining conditions.

[48] Para 3(1) Sch. 4ZA FA 2003

Probably of most practical importance is that if an individual is replacing their main residence, the 3% higher rates will not be applied regardless of the individual holding interests in additional dwellings.

When the 3% higher rates will apply

ALL conditions A-D must be met in order for the 3% higher rates to apply	
Condition A is that the chargeable consideration is £40,000 or more.[49]	✓
Condition B the interest in the dwelling purchased is either not subject to a lease or, if it is subject to a lease, the lease has no more than 21 years to expiry at the date of the transaction.[50]	✓
Condition C is that that the purchaser owns a major interest in another dwelling, valued at more than £40,000 and that dwelling is not subject to a lease which has more than 21 years remaining.[51]	✓
Condition D is that that the dwelling being purchased is **not** replacing the purchaser's only or main residence.[52]	✓

Conditions A and B are relatively straightforward. However, there are a few things that we should bear in mind when considering conditions C and D.

Condition C – Practical considerations

The purchaser owns a major interest in another dwelling, valued at more than £40,000 and that dwelling is not subject to a lease which has more than 21 years remaining.

Let's look at what constitutes an 'interest in a dwelling':

An interest in a dwelling outside of England and Northern Ireland is counted. Consideration of foreign jurisdiction's land law may be required	✓
Mixed-use properties which include an interest in a dwelling (note this is for condition C purposes only, as the higher rates do not apply to the acquisition of mixed-use properties)	✓
Previously gifted interest in a dwelling will be counted	✓
Interests inherited in the last three years will not be counted if the beneficiary and any spouse or civil partner's combined interest does not exceed 50% of the dwelling[53]	✗

---

[49] Para 3(2) Schedule 4ZA FA 2003

[50] Para 3(3) Schedule 4ZA FA 2003

[51] Para 3(4) Schedule 4ZA FA 2003

[52] Para 3(5) Schedule 4ZA FA 2003

[53] Para 16 Schedule 4ZA FA 2003

An interest in a former home retained by a divorcée or ex-civil partner under a court order will not count provided certain conditions are satisfied[54]	✕
Issues of minor children's interests being afforded to their parents and the interests of life tenants in IIP trusts require further consideration for the purposes of Condition C	⚠
There are special rules for applying Condition C in respect of interests held by a partnership which will require further consideration in such cases[55]	⚠

Valuation issues

- ***For the purpose of this valuation,*** it is the market value of the interest owned or treated as owned by the individual in the dwelling. Any debt attaching to the property is disregarded when calculating market value
- The valuation includes the dwelling itself, the gardens and grounds (including buildings and structures in the garden or grounds) and any other land that subsists for the benefit of the dwelling
- Each dwelling owned should be looked at separately. Several interests below this value which add up to £40,000 or more will not cause Condition C to be met
- Joint ownership shares in dwellings must be pro-rated and if the joint owner's interest exceeds £40,000, condition C will be satisfied

Example:

Zara is purchasing a new dwelling and holds three small terraced houses with a combined value of £100,000.

Each individual property is valued at less than £40,000 therefore the 3% rates do not apply.

Example:

Alexa is purchasing a new dwelling and holds a 25% interest in a property which is valued at £125,000 for the entire property.

Alexa's interest in the property does not exceed £40,000 therefore the 3% rates do not apply.

---

[54] Para 9B Schedule 4ZA FA 2003

[55] Para 14 Schedule 4ZA FA 2003

Legal v beneficial ownership

HMRC accept that where an individual has no beneficial interest in a dwelling, it will not be counted for the purposes of Condition C. It is required to be evidenced in writing. *See HMRC Manual SDLTM09785.*

Example:

Blake is purchasing a new dwelling. In order to facilitate Blake's brother obtaining a mortgage for his home purchase, Blake was listed on the title deeds of that property. Blake has no beneficial entitlement in the property and this was documented at the time of purchase.

The 3% rates will not apply.

Transaction involving increasing a share of a dwelling

The interest held must be an interest in another dwelling. A current interest owned in the same dwelling in which a major interest has been purchased will not, on its own, cause Condition C to be met.

FA 2018 introduced new rules disapplying the higher rates involving increases of shares in a purchaser's main residence, provided certain conditions are satisfied[56].

Condition C – Planning Point

Consider the transfer of ownership of Condition C properties to other individuals, limited company or a trust prior to completion.

SDLT and other tax implications should be considered carefully before any action is taken.

Example:

Colin is buying a property for £600,000. Colin also owns an investment property valued at £200,000.

If the investment is held at the date of purchasing the new property, the 3% higher rates will apply and the SDLT will be £38,000. If the 3% rates didn't apply, the SDLT would be £20,000.

[56] Para 7A Schedule 4ZA FA 2003

Colin transfers the investment property to a limited company prior to purchasing the new property. Condition C is now no longer satisfied, therefore the 3% rates do not apply.

However, as the purchaser is a company connected to Colin, S53 FA 2003 applies to apply a deemed market value chargeable consideration to the transaction, incurring an SDLT charge of £7,500.

Result:

The total SDLT cost is £27,500. The transfer to the limited company provides a saving of £10,500.

The practical and other tax implications should be considered before implementing any planning.

Condition D

The dwelling being purchased is <u>not</u> replacing the purchaser's only or main residence

In respect of condition D, there are two situations in which a purchase of a dwelling will be a replacement of a main residence

1. Where the disposal occurred before, or on the day of the purchase[57] and
2. Where the purchase happens first and then the disposal happens later.[58]

Let's look at both of these scenarios in turn.

Case 1 - Disposal occurring before or on the same day as the acquisition of the new property

In respect of disposals which occurred before or on the same day as the purchase of the new dwelling, <u>ALL</u> the following conditions must be satisfied[59]:

On the effective date of the transaction ("the transaction concerned") the purchaser intends the purchased dwelling to be the purchaser's only or **main residence**	✓
In another land transaction ("the previous transaction") whose effective date was the same as or before the effective date of the transaction concerned, the purchaser or the purchaser's spouse or civil partner at the time **disposed of a major interest** in another dwelling ("the sold dwelling")	✓

[57] Para 6 Schedule 4ZA FA 2003
[58] Para 7 Schedule 4ZA FA 2003
[59] Para 3 (6) Schedule 4ZA FA 2003

Immediately after the effective date of the previous transaction, neither the purchaser nor the purchaser's spouse or civil partner had a major interest in the sold dwelling	✓
At any time in the **three years** before the effective date of the transaction concerned the sold dwelling was the purchaser's only or main residence	✓
At no time during the period beginning with the effective date of the previous transaction and ending with the effective date of the transaction concerned has the purchaser or the purchaser's spouse or civil partner acquired a major interest in any other dwelling with the intention of it being the purchaser's only or main residence	✓

If the above conditions are satisfied, the purchase will be a replacement main residence and therefore the 3% higher rates will not apply as condition D is not satisfied.

Example:

Devendra is purchasing a new main residence. On the same day, Devendra will dispose of his previous main residence in which he has lived since its purchase five years ago. Devendra also holds a residential investment property.

The 3% higher rates will not apply in this instance, as the new purchase qualifies a replacement main residence.

Example:

Eric and Frances are married and are purchasing their new main residence. The former main residence is held in Eric's sole name. Frances owns a residential investment property.

Eric and Frances are joint purchasers, therefore both must satisfy all conditions A – D for the 3% higher rates to apply.

Eric is purchasing a new main residence and has disposed of an interest held in a previous main residence. Condition D is not satisfied therefore if sole purchaser, 3% higher rates would not apply.

Frances does not hold an interest in the previous main residence, but her spouse has disposed of an interest in a property which she occupied as her main residence. Condition D is not satisfied.

Condition D is not satisfied for both Eric and Frances, therefore 3% higher rates will not apply to the purchase of the new home.

If Eric and Frances were not married, Frances would not meet the conditions to be a replacement main residence so that condition D would be satisfied, and the 3% higher rates would apply to the joint purchase of the new home. In such a case, consideration could be given to Frances acquiring an in interest in the property prior to any future disposal. The SDLT and other tax implications should be considered before any action is taken.

Case 2 - Disposal occurring after the acquisition of the new property

In respect of disposals which occur after the purchase of the new dwelling, the purchased dwelling will become a replacement for the purchaser's only or main residence if ALL the following conditions are satisfied[60]:

On the effective date of the transaction ("the transaction concerned") the purchaser intended the purchased dwelling to be the purchaser's only or **main residence**	✓
In another land transaction whose effective date is during the period of **three years** beginning with the day after the effective date of the transaction concerned, the purchaser or the purchaser's spouse or civil partner disposes of a major interest in another dwelling ("the sold dwelling")	✓
Immediately after the effective date of that other land transaction, neither the purchaser nor the purchaser's spouse or civil partner has a major interest in the sold dwelling	✓
At any time during the period of **three years** ending with the effective date of the transaction concerned the sold dwelling was the purchaser's only or main residence	✓

In summary, there is a replacement of a main residence if, at the time of a purchase, the transaction was a higher-rates transaction and in the following three years, the purchaser sells a previous main residence. The previous main residence must have been the main residence of the purchaser at some time during the three years before the purchase of the new main residence.

In this scenario, the 3% higher rates of SDLT will be applied to the purchase of the new main residence but a reclaim of the additional tax will be available within prescribed time limits. We'll look at reclaims in more detail later in this chapter.

[60] Schedule 4ZA Para 7 FA 2003

Example:

Guillem is purchasing a new main residence but does not find a buyer for his previous main residence until 1 year after the purchase of the new main residence.

The 3% higher rates will apply to the purchase of the new main residence but the amount attributable to the additional 3% can be reclaimed once the previous main residence is sold.

Example:

Harry purchased a main residence and paid the 3% higher rates as he held an additional dwelling at the time of sale. One year later, Harry disposes of the additional dwelling which has always been held as an investment property.

Harry cannot reclaim the additional 3% tax paid because he did not dispose of a main residence.

Condition D– Practical Considerations

There are two components required to be a replacement of a purchaser's main residence:

1. There must be a disposal of a major interest in the purchaser's or their spouse or civil partner's previous main residence (the test for the old dwelling is a question of objective fact); *and*
2. The dwelling acquired must be intended to be occupied as the individual's only or main residence (the test in respect of the new dwelling purchased is a question of intention at the time of purchase).

With regard to what constitutes a 'main residence', *Frost v Feltham (55TC10) & HMRC Manual SDLTM09812* includes a helpful list of factors to consider:

- *If the individual is married or in a civil partnership, where does the family spend its time?*
- *If the individual has children, where do they go to school?*
- *At which residence is the individual registered to vote?*
- *Where is the individual's place of work?*
- *How is each residence furnished?*
- *Which address is used for correspondence?*

- *Where is the individual registered with a doctor / dentist?*
- *At which address is the individual's car registered and insured?*
- *Which address is the main residence for council tax?*

Renting a new main residence in the time between disposal and purchase will not prevent the purchase from being a replacement of a main residence, unless the period of the tenancy agreed is more than seven years.

Condition D – planning point

The disposal of the previous main residence does not have to be by way of sale. It could be:

- by way of a gift,
- transferred to a limited company or trust or
- transferred as part of a divorce settlement

SDLT and other tax implications should be considered carefully before any action is taken.

Example

Isobel purchased her new main residence and paid the 3% higher rates, because at the effective date Isobel retained an interest in her previous main residence.

One year later, Isobel gifts the previous main residence to her adult son. The property was unencumbered, therefore there was no chargeable consideration and no SDLT arising on the gift.

Isobel can make a reclaim for the 3% additional tax paid on the purchase of her new main residence.

Replacement Main Residence - Claiming a repayment

If a previous main residence is sold within three years of paying higher rates on a new main residence purchase, a refund can be claimed by making an amendment to the original return.

HMRC have confirmed that individuals who purchased their new home on or after 1 January 2017 and are unable to sell their previous home within three years due to the impact of Covid-19, may still be eligible for a refund.

Repayments need to be claimed within 12 months of the sale of the previous main residence or within one year of the filing of the return on the new property, whichever is later.

Companies and non-individual purchasers

Companies

Where the purchaser is not an individual, the higher rates will apply if conditions A and B are met:

Condition A is that the chargeable consideration is £40,000 or more	✓
Condition B the interest in the dwelling purchased is either not subject to a lease or, if it is subject to a lease, the lease has no more than 21 years to expiry at the date of the transaction.	✓

Example

Jelton Ltd purchases a dwelling costing £100,000. This is the company's first property acquisition.

The 3% higher rates will apply.

Trusts

The treatment is dependent on whether the acquisition is by trustees of:

- a bare trust
- a trust with life or income interests or
- any other trust, typically a discretionary trust or accumulation & maintenance trust

Let's look a little closer at each of these situations.

Bare trust

A trustee is a trustee of a bare trust if the beneficiary or beneficiaries are absolutely entitled to the property against the trustees.

The trustee(s) of a bare trust are ignored for the purposes of determining whether a purchase is subject to the higher rates, and the absolute beneficiary or beneficiaries are treated as the purchaser(s).

A trust with life or income interests

A trustee is a trustee of a life interest trust if some beneficiary is entitled to either[61]:

occupy the dwelling for life, *or*	✓
the income earned in respect of the dwelling	✓

It does not matter if one or more than one beneficiary has the entitlement to occupy or entitlement to income.

On a purchase by a trustee of a trust for life or income interests, whether the higher rates apply is determined as if any beneficiaries with the interests above were the purchaser or purchasers and the trustee was not the purchaser.

So, if the beneficiary for life is an individual and the purchase is of a single dwelling, the trustee must consider whether the individual, and not the trustee, meets Conditions C and D.

If the beneficiary owns another interest in a dwelling worth £40,000 or more, and not subject to a 21-year lease, then it will be a higher-rates transaction unless the trustees' purchase is a replacement of the beneficiary's main residence.

Any other type of trust

Where a person purchases a dwelling as a trustee and the trust is neither a bare trust nor a trust for life or income, the trustee is liable to the higher rates in the same situation as a company purchaser[62] above.

That is, where a purchased dwelling meets Condition A (consideration paid is £40,000 or more) and Condition B (not subject to a 21-year lease), the higher rates will apply.

Example

The trustees of a discretionary trust are purchasing a property to be one of the beneficiary's main residence. The trust holds no other dwellings.

The 3% higher rates apply.

---

[61] Para 10 Schedule 4ZA FA 2003

[62] Para 13 Schedule 4ZA FA 2003

Single Dwelling Transactions Checklist

Transactions which do not attract 3% rates	
Non-residential or mixed-use properties	✗
Transactions where the consideration is less than £40,000	✗
Freehold or leasehold interests with a term of less than 7 years to run on the effective date	✗
Spouses/civil partners purchasing from one another – transactions between one spouse/civil partner and the other (who are living together) are not higher rate transactions	✗
High value residential property transactions where the 15% charge applies. Care required where purchase includes a chargeable interest that is not a higher threshold interest	✗
Most purchases of caravans, houseboats and mobile homes	✗
Is it a higher rate transaction?	
Sole purchaser meets all the specified conditions	✓
Joint purchasers meet all the specified conditions	✓
Spouses/civil partners purchasing alone - where one spouse/civil partner is purchasing alone, and the other spouse/civil partner meets the conditions for the higher rates, the transaction will be deemed to be a higher rates transaction even if the purchasing spouse/civil partner does not satisfy the conditions.	✓
Summary of conditions A - D	
Condition A is that the chargeable consideration is £40,000 or more.[63]	✓
Condition B the interest in the dwelling purchased is either not subject to a lease or, if it is subject to a lease, the lease has no more than 21 years to expiry at the date of the transaction.[64]	✓
Condition C is that that the purchaser owns a major interest in another dwelling, valued at more than £40,000 and that dwelling is not subject to a lease which has more than 21 years remaining.[65]	✓
Condition D is that that the dwelling being purchased is <u>**not**</u> replacing the purchaser's only or main residence.[66]	✓

[63] Para 3(2) Schedule 4ZA FA 2003
[64] Para 3(3) Schedule 4ZA FA 2003
[65] Para 3(4) Schedule 4ZA FA 2003
[66] Para 3(5) Schedule 4ZA FA 2003

Individual purchaser(s)	
Is the purchaser an individual?	✓
Are ALL conditions A – D met?	✓
3% higher rates apply	
Are ALL conditions A – D met?	✗
3% rates will not apply	
Company purchaser(s)	
Is the purchaser a company?	✓
Are conditions A & B met?	✓
3% higher rates apply	
Are conditions A & B met?	✗
3% rates will not apply	
Trustee purchaser(s)	
Is the purchaser a trustee of a settlement?	✓
Is the settlement a **bare trust?**	✓
The beneficiary is treated as the purchaser. Are conditions A - D met for the beneficiary?	✓
3% higher rates apply	
Are conditions A - D met for the beneficiary?	✗
3% rates will not apply	
Is the settlement a settlement with **life or income interest?**	✓
The beneficiary is treated as the purchaser. Are conditions A - D met for the beneficiary?	✓
3% higher rates apply	
Are conditions A - D met for the beneficiary?	✗
3% rates will not apply	
Is the settlement **any other type of settlement** (including discretionary and A&M trusts)?	✓
Treated like a corporate purchase. Are conditions A & B met?	✓
3% higher rates apply	
Are conditions A & B met?	✗
3% rates will not apply	

Chapter Eight
3% Higher Rates for Additional Dwellings – Multiple Dwelling Transactions

At a Glance

There are different rules for the acquisition of two or more dwellings, depending on whether the purchaser is an individual or not.

For individuals, there are two separate tests to determine if the 3% higher rates apply. These are dependent on how many properties met the prescribed 3 conditions. Concept of 'subsidiary dwelling' very important.

For companies, if at least one of the dwellings meet two prescribed conditions, the 3% rates will apply.

For trustees, it depends on the type of trust.

Introduction

As with single dwelling transactions, there are various conditions (which differ depending on whether the purchaser is an individual or a company) that must be met for the 3% higher SDLT rate to apply. In this chapter, we'll outline these conditions and look at how they're applied in practice.

Individuals

The application of the higher rates differs when an individual purchases two or more dwellings. Moreover, there are two separate tests to determine whether the higher rates will be applied depending on how many of the dwellings meet conditions A-C. These conditions are also different to the conditions that apply when an individual purchases one dwelling.

Conditions A – C can be summarised as follows:

Condition A is that the chargeable consideration for the purchased dwelling (attributable on a just and reasonable basis) is £40,000 or more.[67]	✓
Condition B is that the purchased dwelling is not subject to a sub-lease which has more than 21 years to run on the day of purchase.[68]	✓
Condition C is that the purchased dwelling is not **subsidiary** to any of the other purchased dwellings.[69]	✓

Subsidiary dwelling

Condition C is met if the dwelling is not subsidiary to another of the purchased dwellings and was included in the legislation to ensure 'granny flats' did not come within the scope of the higher rates.

The test is two-pronged in determining whether a dwelling ('the subsidiary dwelling') is subsidiary to another dwelling ('the principal dwelling').

It must be located in the same grounds or building **AND**	✓
The principal dwelling and the garden and grounds attributable to that principal dwelling must be at least two-thirds of the value of the entire transaction	✓

There can be more than one subsidiary dwelling purchased at the same time as a principal dwelling, but the principal dwelling must always be at least two-thirds of the transaction value.

> ***Example:***
>
> Kirsten is purchasing a property with a self-contained granny flat for £750,000. The main house is valued at £600,000. The granny flat is in the same building and the main house is valued at more than two-thirds of the total consideration.
>
> The granny flat is a subsidiary dwelling.
>
> If the main house was valued below £500,000, the granny flat would not be counted as a subsidiary dwelling.

[67] Para 5(2) Sch. 4 ZA FA 2003

[68] Para 5(3) Sch. 4 ZA FA 2003

[69] Para 5(4) Sch. 4 ZA FA 2003

Example:

Leo buys two flats in the same block, one for himself (residence) and one for his mother. Leo's flat is worth £500,000 and his mother's flat is worth £250,000. The lower valued property is a subsidiary dwelling.

Martin buys two houses in the same street: one for himself (residence) and one for his mother. Martin's house is worth £500,000 and his mother's has a value of £250,000. The lower valued property is **not** a subsidiary dwelling, as the property is not in the same building or garden and grounds.

Example:

Nish is purchasing a property with a separate cottage situated in the grounds which he intends to rent out as a holiday let. The total consideration is £750,000 and the main property is valued at £600,000. The cottage is in the same grounds as the main house and the main house is valued at more than two thirds of the total consideration.

The cottage is a subsidiary dwelling.

The two separate tests are based on the number of dwellings satisfying conditions A – C

Where at least two of the purchased dwellings meet all conditions A – C[70] and	✓✓
Where only one of the purchased dwellings meet all conditions A – C[71]	✓

Test One - Where at least TWO of the purchased dwellings meet all conditions A – C

Where an individual purchases a major interest in two or more dwellings, the higher rates of SDLT will be applied if at least two of the purchased dwellings meet conditions A, B and C.

Therefore, if there are two or more 'principal' (non-subsidiary) dwellings which are valued at £40,000 or more and are not reversionary on a lease with more than 21 years to run, the higher rates will automatically apply.

In such cases, it is irrelevant if the individual holds additional properties or if they are replacing a main residence.

[70] Para 5 Schedule 4ZA FA 2003

[71] Para 6 Schedule 4ZA FA 2003

Example:

Oscar is a property developer and is buying 5 properties from the same vendor for £600,000 in total. Oscar owns no other property interests.

As none of the properties will be subsidiary, all 5 properties will satisfy conditions A-C and therefore the 3% higher rates apply.

Test two – Where only ONE of the purchased dwellings meet all conditions A - C

Where only **one** of the purchased dwellings meets all conditions A – C, the higher rates will only apply if **both** the following conditions are also satisfied:

The purchased dwelling which meets the conditions is not a replacement main residence	✓
At the end of the day that is the effective date of the transaction – the purchaser has a major interest in a dwelling other than one of the purchased dwellings, – that interest has a market value of £40,000 or more, and – that interest is not reversionary on a lease which has an unexpired term of more than 21 years.	✓

Example:

Penny is purchasing a property with a self-contained granny flat for £750,000. The main house is valued at £600,000. The granny flat is in the same building and the main house is valued at more than two-thirds of the total consideration.

As the granny flat is a subsidiary dwelling, only one of the dwellings meets all conditions A – C.

Penny has recently sold her former main residence in order to facilitate the purchase of her property.

As the 'principal' property is replacing her main residence, the above condition is not satisfied, so the 3% higher rates will not be applied.

Interaction with Multiple Dwellings Relief

Where two or more dwellings are being purchased, consideration should be given to claiming MDR. In these circumstances, it still remains to be determined whether the 3% higher rates will apply to the MDR calculation.

Test one circumstances - where at least TWO of the purchased dwellings meet all conditions A – C

Example:

Quentin, a property developer, is planning to purchase a block of 15 flats for the total consideration of £1.7m. Each flat is of a similar value.

Although all the flats are within the same building, all the flats will be considered to be non-subsidiary dwellings by virtue of their valuations. Therefore the 3% higher rates will apply as all 15 properties will satisfy conditions A-C, giving rise to SDLT of £168,750. This is the figure provided when this information is inputted in HMRC's SDLT calculator.

However, S116 (7) FA 2003 specifically provides that where **six or more** dwellings are purchased, they will not be treated as residential property. Accordingly, the rates at Table B (non-residential) should be applied, resulting in the total tax payable of £74,500.

As two or more dwellings are purchased, a claim for Multiple Dwellings Relief could also be considered.

Relevant consideration (£)	SDLT rate	SDLT (£)
113,333	3%	4,000
X 15 properties (£1,700,000)		**£51,000**
1% of total consideration check		*£17,000*

Therefore, a claim for MDR would result in SDLT payable of £51,000, resulting in a saving of £117,750 compared to the quoted amount on HMRC's calculator.

Test two circumstances - where only ONE of the purchased dwellings meet all conditions A - C

It is important to note that the fact that a dwelling is treated as subsidiary for the purposes of the 3% higher rates (i.e. in effect, one single property), does not preclude MDR from applying. Provided each dwelling satisfies the conditions to be treated as separate dwellings, MDR may still be claimed.[72]

Example:

Rachel and Sophie are purchasing a replacement main residence for £1,250,000. The property has a self-contained annex with kitchen, bathroom, bedroom and living space and a lockable door.

[72] HMRC Stamp Duty Land Tax Manual – SDLTM09755

The estate agent provided a valuation split of £1,000,000 for the main property and £250,000 for the annex.

The annex is treated as a subsidiary dwelling as the annex is within the same building and the main property is more than two-thirds of the total consideration.

The second test applies as only one property meets conditions A-C. As the property qualifies as replacement main residence, the 3% higher rates will not apply and the SDLT is £68,750 by applying the standard rates at Table A.

On the basis that the annex is capable of independent living and affords a sufficient degree of privacy, the annex will be treated as a separate dwelling for the purposes of MDR.

Relevant consideration (£)	SDLT rate	SDLT (£)
125,000	0%	Nil
125.000	2%	2,500
375,000	5%	18,750
625,000		21,250
X 2 properties (£1,250,000)		**£42,500**
1% of total consideration check		*£12.500*

Therefore, a claim for MDR would result in SDLT payable of £42,500, resulting in a saving of £26,250.

Companies and non-individual purchasers

Companies

Where the purchaser is not an individual and the subject matter of the transaction consists of a major interest in two or more dwellings, the higher rates will apply if **at least one** of the dwellings meet conditions A and B:

Condition A is that the chargeable consideration is £40,000 or more	✓
Condition B is that the interest in the dwelling purchased is either not subject to a lease or, if it is subject to a lease, the lease has no more than 21 years to expiry at the date of the transaction.	✓

Example

TDT Ltd purchases two dwellings costing £100,000 each.

The 3% higher rates will apply.

Trusts

The treatment is dependent on whether the acquisition is by trustees of:

- a bare trust
- a trust with life or income interests or
- any other trust, typically a discretionary trust or accumulation & maintenance trust.

Bare trust

A trustee is a trustee of a bare trust if the beneficiary or beneficiaries are absolutely entitled to the property against the trustees.

The trustee(s) of a bare trust are ignored for the purposes of determining whether a purchase is subject to the higher rates, and the absolute beneficiary or beneficiaries are treated as the purchaser(s).

Therefore, consideration of the rules applicable to individuals acquiring multiple dwellings (discussed above) will be required for the beneficiary/beneficiaries of the bare trust.

A trust with life or income interests

A trustee is a trustee of a life interest trust if some beneficiary is entitled to either[73]:

occupy the dwelling for life, *or*	✓
the income earned in respect of the dwelling	✓

It does not matter if one or more than one beneficiary has the entitlement to occupy or entitlement to income.

On a purchase by a trustee of a trust for life or income interests, whether the higher rates apply is determined as if any beneficiaries with the interests above were the purchaser or purchasers and the trustee was not the purchaser.

Therefore, consideration of the rules applicable to individuals acquiring multiple dwellings (discussed above) will be required for the beneficiary/beneficiaries of the trust with life or income interests.

---

[73] Para 10 Schedule 4ZA FA 2003

Any other type of trust

Where a person purchases more than one dwellings as a trustee and the trust is neither a bare trust nor a trust for life or income, the trustee is liable to the higher rates in the same situation as a company purchaser[74] above.

That is, where **at least one** of the purchased dwellings meets Condition A (consideration paid is £40,000 or more) and Condition B (not subject to a 21-year lease), the higher rates will apply.

[74] Para 13 Schedule 4ZA FA 2003

Multiple Dwelling Transactions Checklist

Transactions which do not attract 3% rates	
Non-residential or mixed-use properties	✗
Transactions where the consideration is less than £40,000	✗
Freehold or leasehold interests with a term of less than 7 years to run on the effective date	✗
Spouses/civil partners purchasing from one another – transactions between one spouse/civil partner and the other (who are living together) are not higher rate transactions	✗
High value residential property transactions where the 15% charge applies. Care required where purchase includes a chargeable interest that is not a higher threshold interest	✗
Most purchases of caravans, houseboats and mobile homes	✗
Is it a higher rate transaction?	
Sole purchaser meets all the specified conditions	✓
Joint purchasers meet all the specified conditions	✓
Spouses/civil partners purchasing alone - where one spouse/civil partner is purchasing alone, and the other spouse/civil partner meets the conditions for the higher rates, the transaction will be deemed to be a higher rates transaction even if the purchasing spouse/civil partner does not satisfy the conditions.	✓
Summary of conditions A - C	
Condition A is that the chargeable consideration for the purchased dwelling (attributable on a just and reasonable basis) is £40,000 or more.[75]	✓
Condition B is that the purchased dwelling is not subject to a sub-lease which has more than 21 years to run on the day of purchase.[76]	✓
Condition C is that the purchased dwelling is not subsidiary to any of the other purchased dwellings.[77]	✓
Is there a subsidiary dwelling?	
It must be located in the same grounds or building **AND**	✓
The principal dwelling and the garden and grounds attributable to that principal dwelling must be at least two thirds of the value of the entire transaction	✓

[75] Para 5(2) Sch. 4 ZA FA 2003

[76] Para 5(3) Sch. 4 ZA FA 2003

[77] Para 5(4) Sch. 4 ZA FA 2003

<table>
<tr><th colspan="2">Individual purchaser(s)</th></tr>
<tr><td colspan="2">Test One - Where at least TWO of the purchased dwellings meet all conditions A – C</td></tr>
<tr><td>Is the purchaser an individual?</td><td>✓</td></tr>
<tr><td>Do at least two of the dwellings meet all conditions A - C?</td><td>✓</td></tr>
<tr><td>3% higher rates apply</td><td></td></tr>
<tr><td>Do at least two of the dwellings meet all conditions A - C?</td><td>✗</td></tr>
<tr><td>Go to Test Two</td><td>?</td></tr>
<tr><td colspan="2">Test Two – Where only ONE of the purchased dwellings meet all conditions A - C</td></tr>
<tr><td>Is the purchaser an individual?</td><td>✓</td></tr>
<tr><td>Does only one of the dwellings meet conditions A – C?</td><td>✓</td></tr>
<tr><td>Are BOTH of the following conditions met?
1. The purchased dwelling which meets the conditions is not a replacement main residence
2. At the end of the day that is the effective date of the transaction
– the purchaser has a major interest in a dwelling other than one of the purchased dwellings
– that interest has a market value of £40,000 or more, and
– that interest is not reversionary on a lease which has an unexpired term of more than 21 years.</td><td>✓</td></tr>
<tr><td>3% rates will apply</td><td></td></tr>
<tr><td>Are Both of the above conditions met?</td><td>✗</td></tr>
<tr><td>3% rates will not apply</td><td></td></tr>
<tr><th colspan="2">Company purchaser(s)</th></tr>
<tr><td>Is the purchaser a company?</td><td>✓</td></tr>
<tr><td>Are conditions A & B met for at least one of the purchased dwellings?</td><td>✓</td></tr>
<tr><td>3% higher rates apply</td><td></td></tr>
<tr><td>Are conditions A & B met for at least one of the purchased dwellings?</td><td>✗</td></tr>
<tr><td>3% rates will not apply</td><td></td></tr>
<tr><th colspan="2">Trustee purchaser(s)</th></tr>
<tr><td>Is the purchaser a trustee of a settlement?</td><td>✓</td></tr>
<tr><td>Is the settlement a bare trust?</td><td>✓</td></tr>
<tr><td>The beneficiary is treated as the purchaser.
Refer to individual purchaser checklist above.</td><td>?</td></tr>
<tr><td>Is the settlement a settlement with life or income interest?</td><td>✓</td></tr>
<tr><td>The beneficiary is treated as the purchaser.
Refer to individual purchaser checklist above.</td><td>?</td></tr>
<tr><td>Is the settlement any other type of settlement (including discretionary and A&M trusts)?</td><td>✓</td></tr>
</table>

Treated like a corporate purchase. Are conditions A & B met for at least one of the purchased dwellings?	✓
3% higher rates apply	
Are conditions A & B met for at least one of the purchased dwellings?	✗
3% rates will not apply	

Chapter Nine
15% Higher Rate for Acquisitions of Residential Property by Certain Non-Natural Persons

At a Glance

A 15% flat rate applies to purchases of single dwellings valued at £500,000 or more, where the purchaser is a company or other non-natural person.

Separate calculations are required where the transaction involves:

- dwellings costing £500,000 or more and dwellings not exceeding this value
- dwellings costing £500,000 or more and non-residential properties.

There are a number of specific reliefs available which disapply the 15% rate, including where the property is acquired in the business of letting, trading in or redeveloping properties.

Introduction

For transactions with an effective date on or after 21 March 2012, a flat rate of 15% applies to the purchase of a 'higher threshold interest' in residential property where the consideration exceeds the higher rate threshold, and where the purchaser is a 'non-natural person'.

The 15% rate is detailed in Schedule 4A FA 2003, which formed part of a package of measures to combat the 'enveloping' of high value residential property and its perceived mischiefs.

This chapter clarifies key terms and details when the rate will apply (and when it will not).

When the 15% will Apply

A **'high-value residential transaction'** will occur, and thus the 15% rate will apply to the whole of the chargeable consideration, when a **'higher threshold interest' is** purchased by a **'non-natural person'**.

Higher threshold interest is an interest in a single dwelling if the chargeable consideration is attributable to that interest exceeds £500,000.	✓
Non-natural persons include companies, partnerships which include a company as a member, or collective investment schemes[78]. However, this does not include a company acting in its capacity as a trustee of a settlement[79].	✓

Further application of these rules:

- **Joint purchasers:** applies where a higher threshold interest is acquired by two or more purchasers acting jointly, and at least one of those purchasers is one of the entities above[80]
- **Leases:** applies where the premium on the grant of a lease exceeds the higher threshold interest, i.e. £500,000. The normal rules on rent apply.
- **Partnerships:** Para 6 of Schedule 4A FA 2003 details the application of the 15% rate to transactions to which Part 3 of Schedule 15 (Special Partnership Transactions) applies. See Chapter 15 for discussion on partnership transactions.

High-Value Residential Transactions: Practical Implications

If the main subject matter of a transaction consists entirely of 'higher threshold interests', then the transaction is a 'high-value residential transaction'.

If the main subject matter of a transaction includes a chargeable interest other than a 'higher threshold interest' then the transaction ('the primary transaction') is treated as two separate chargeable transactions consisting of:

- a transaction whose subject matter is all the 'higher threshold interests'; *and*
- a transaction consisting of the remainder of the subject-matter of the 'primary transaction'.

For example:

- an acquisition of a large dwelling valued at over £500,000, plus a second dwelling worth less than £500,000
- the acquisition of a mixed-use property which includes within it a dwelling with an apportioned consideration which exceeds £500,000.

---

[78] Para 3 (3) Schedule 4A FA 2003

[79] Para 3 (4) Schedule 4A FA 2003

[80] Para 3 (5) Schedule 4A FA 2003

The total consideration must be apportioned on a just and reasonable basis, so that the higher threshold interests attract the 15% higher rate and the remaining interests attract SDLT at normal rates.

The acquisitions are not treated as linked transactions and the amount of tax due in respect of the acquisition of the interest(s) that are not higher threshold interests will be determined by the chargeable consideration apportioned to those interests, not the chargeable consideration for the primary transaction.

Higher Threshold Interest: Practical Implications

A higher threshold interest is an interest in a single dwelling if the chargeable consideration attributable to that interest exceeds £500,000.

Therefore, the rate will apply if the interest in a single dwelling exceeds £500,000.

Schedule 4A provides the definition of a dwelling[81] as follows:

It is used or suitable for use as a single dwelling, See *P N Bewley Ltd v Revenue and Customs Commissioners [2019] UKFTT 65 (TC) for discussion on what constitutes 'suitable for use' a dwelling for these purposes.*	✓
It is in the process of being constructed or adapted for such use.	✓
Land that is, or is to be, occupied or enjoyed with a dwelling as a garden or grounds (including any building or structure on that land) is taken to be part of that dwelling. However, a transaction of such land without the purchase of the actual dwelling will not be liable to the 15%.	✓
Off-plan purchases can also count as a dwelling where certain conditions are met	✓
A building or part of a building used for the purposes specified in S116 (2) [which are normally treated as dwellings for SDLT purposes] or (3) FA 2003 [which are not normally treated as dwellings for SDLT purposes] is not used as a dwelling for the purposes of the 15% rate.	✓

Detailed HMRC guidance

SDLTM00380 – SDLTM00400 (Dated 1 October 2019)	Guidance on what constitutes a dwelling, and guidance on the terms 'suitable for use' and 'in the process of being constructed or adapted for use as a dwelling'.
SDLTM00440 to SDLTM00480 (Dated 25 June 2019)	Guidance on the meaning of garden or grounds for the definition of residential property.

[81] Para 7 Schedule 4A FA 2003

SDLTM00410 – SDLTM00430 (Dated 1 October 2019)	Guidance on how to determine the number of dwellings forming part of a land transaction.
SDLTM9520	Where a building includes a number of dwellings (for example, a block of flats), all the dwellings in the building will be treated as being in the process of being constructed when this test is met, not when construction of the individual dwelling is commenced. This principle applies even if the ground floor is intended for non-residential use (for example, where the building consists of a shop with flats above).

When the 15% will Not Apply (Specific Exemptions)

Schedule 4A provides a number of specific exemptions.

Business of letting, trading in or redeveloping properties[82]	✗
Relief is denied/withdrawn where a non-qualifying individual occupies the property[83] within three years of the effective date. In practice, this typically gives rise to an issue if the shareholder/director of the company or a family member of said individual occupies the property during the first three years after purchase. The relief is withdrawn even if the occupier pays a market value rent. HMRC are increasingly raising enquiries into this area.	⚠
Trades involving making a dwelling available to the public[84]	✗
Financial institutions acquiring dwellings in the course of lending[85]	✗
Acquisition under a regulated home reversion plan[86]	✗
Dwellings for occupation by certain employees etc of a relievable business[87]	✗
Acquisition by management company of flat for occupation by caretaker[88]	✗
Farmhouses[89]	✗

[82] Para 5 Schedule 4A FA 2003

[83] Para 5A Schedule 4A FA 2003

[84] Para 5B Schedule 4A FA 2003

[85] Para 5C Schedule 4A FA 2003

[86] Para 5CA Schedule 4A FA 2003

[87] Para 5D – 5E Schedule 4A FA 2003

[88] Para 5EA Schedule 4A FA 2003

[89] Para 5F Schedule 4A FA 2003

It is important to note that the above reliefs are not automatic and must be claimed on the SDLT return.	⚠
Furthermore, the legislation provides for the withdrawal of the specific relief claimed if certain conditions are met. (Paras 5G – 5K and Para 6D – 6H of Schedule 4A FA 2003).	⚠

Example:

Ultan holds the entire shareholding of Vanguard Ltd. Vanguard Ltd purchases a residential property for £550,000 with the view to generate rental income. Vanguard Ltd claims relief on the SDLT return and pays SDLT at the 3% higher rates.

Ultan's personal circumstances change, and he decides to move into the property in the second year following its purchase.

Vanguard Ltd is required to submit a new return and pay the additional SDLT due at a flat rate of 15%.

A building or part of a building used for the purposes specified in S116 (2) or (3) FA 2003 is not used as a dwelling for the purposes of the 15% rate. Therefore, any acquisitions of buildings used for the following will not be within the scope of the 15% charge.

Buildings which are normally treated as dwellings for SDLT purposes	**Does the 15% rate apply?**
Residential accommodation for school pupils	✕
Residential accommodation for students, other than a hall of residence for students in further or higher education	✕
Residential accommodation for members of the armed forces	✕
An institution that is the sole or main residence of at least 90% of its residents and does not fall within any of specified categories of buildings not used as a dwelling (see below)	✕

Buildings which are not normally treated as dwellings for SDLT purposes	Does the 15% rate apply?
A home or other institution providing residential accommodation for children	✗
A hall of residence for students in further or higher education	✗
A home or other institution providing residential accommodation with personal care for persons in need of personal care by reason of old age, disablement, past or present dependence on alcohol or drugs or past or present mental disorder	✗
A hospital or hospice	✗
A prison or similar establishment	✗
A hotel or inn or similar establishment	✗

The legislation provides for certain modifications for cases involving alternative finance arrangements[90].

This is a complex area and one to which HMRC pay particular attention, given the potential revenue take. Specialist advice should be sought in cases of doubt.	

[90] Para 6A -6D Schedule 4A FA 2003

Chapter Ten
Reliefs

At a Glance

Reliefs are available in certain prescribed circumstances to reduce the SDLT exposure.

The reliefs are not automatic and must be claimed on the SDLT return at question 9.

If a relief is not claimed, there is a 12-month timeframe to make an amended return to claim the relief and generate a refund.

Introduction

There are various reliefs available to reduce the SDLT liability arising in a land transaction. This chapter seeks to highlight the available reliefs, whilst chapters 7 to 12 cover the most relevant for conveyancers in further detail.

In an increasingly litigious society, it is extremely important to identify the availability of any reliefs in a land transaction. It should be noted that the application of the reliefs can be complex. It may be advisable to seek professional advice in cases of doubt.

Available SDLT reliefs

First Time Buyers Relief - S57B & Schedule 6ZA FA 2003 See Chapter 11	✓
Multiple Dwellings Relief – Schedule 6B FA 2003 - which broadly operates by restricting the rate of SDLT on the acquisition of a portfolio of residential property by reference to the average price per dwelling See Chapter 12	✓
Sale and leaseback – S57A FA 2003 See Chapter 13	✓
Certain acquisitions of residential property – Schedule 6A FA 2003 • Acquisitions by house-building company from individual acquiring new dwelling[91] • Acquisition by property trader from individual acquiring new dwelling[92] • Acquisition by property trader from personal representatives[93] • Acquisition by property trader from individual where chain of transactions breaks down[94] • Acquisition by employer in case of relocation of employment[95] • Acquisition by property trader in case of relocation of employment[96]	✓
Group Relief – Para 1 Schedule 7 FA 2003 - for transfer of property between corporate entities within the same group	✓
Reconstructions Relief – Para 7 Schedule 7 FA 2003- for corporate demergers	✓
Acquisitions Relief – Para 8 Schedule 7 FA 2003 - available on the acquisition of property that is part of a trading undertaking for the issue of shares which has the effect of restricting the rate of SDLT to 0.5%	✓
Charities Relief - Schedule 8 - for the acquisition of property by charities for charitable purposes	✓
Compulsory purchase to facilitate development - S60 FA 2003	✓
Compliance with planning obligations - S61 FA 2003	✓
Demutualisation of insurance company - S63 FA 2003	✓
Demutualisation of building society - S64 FA 2003	✓
Incorporation of limited liability partnership - S65 FA 2003	✓
Transfers involving public bodies - S66 FA 2003	✓
Reorganisation of parliamentary constituencies - S65 FA 2003	✓

---

91 Para 1 Schedule 6A FA 2003

92 Para 2 Schedule 6A FA 2003

93 Para 3 Schedule 6A FA 2003

94 Para 4 Schedule 6A FA 2003

95 Para 5 Schedule 6A FA 2003

96 Para 6 Schedule 6A FA 2003

Acquisition by bodies established for national purposes etc - S69 FA 2003	✓
Certain acquisitions made by registered social landlords - S71 FA 2003	✓
Alternative property finance: Land sold to financial institution and leased or resold to individual - S71A and S73 FA 2003	✓
Collective enfranchisement by leaseholders - S74 FA 2003	✓
Crofting community right to buy - S75 FA 2003	✓
PAIF seeding relief and COACS seeding relief - SCH7A FA 2003	✓

In all cases, it should be remembered that the reliefs are not automatic and must be claimed on the SDLT return or by way of an amended return (within 12 months).	⚠

Chapter Eleven
Relief for First-Time Buyers

At a Glance

For transactions occurring between 8 July 2020 – 31 March 2021, First -Time Buyers Relief is disapplied.

Reduced rates of SDLT apply for qualifying first-time buyers.

The legislation sets out 4 conditions along with a final proviso which must ALL be satisfied in order to be eligible to claim the relief.

The relief applies to the purchase of residential dwellings only and the property must be purchased with the intention of being the purchaser's only or main residence.

The relief is only available to first-time buyers. The relief will not be available where the purchaser holds or has previously held a dwelling. This includes acquisitions by way of gifts or inheritances.

First time buyers' relief can apply to those buying on a shared ownership basis.

Introduction

First-time buyers can avail of reduced rates of SDLT, but there are qualifying factors that you'll need to be aware of. The legislation sets out four conditions (plus a final proviso) all of which must be satisfied to be eligible for the relief.

In this chapter, we'll look at these conditions in detail, including the practical implications and key things to watch out for.

For transactions occurring between 8 July 2020 – 31 March 2021, First -Time Buyers Relief is disapplied.

Background

First Time Buyers Relief applies to land transactions with an effective date on or after 22 November 2017. S57B & Schedule 6ZA FA 2003 provide relief to first-time buyers where certain conditions are satisfied, so that the following rates are applied.

Relevant consideration	SDLT rate
Up to £300,000	0%
Any remainder (so far as not exceeding £500,000)	5%

In practice

- First-time buyers of homes worth below £300,000 will pay no SDLT
- First-time buyers of properties valued between £300,000 and £500,000 will not pay SDLT on the first £300,000, and a rate of 5% between £300,000 and £500,000
- If the property is valued above £500,000, no relief can be claimed.

Example

Veronica is a first-time buyer and is purchasing a property for £500,000. The SDLT is calculated as follows

Relevant consideration (£)	SDLT rate	SDLT (£)
300,000	0%	Nil
200,000	5%	10,000
500,000		10,000

SDLT on £500,000 at the standard rates would result in a liability of £15,000. Therefore, the relief can provide up to £5,000 of relief for first-time buyers.

The relief is not automatic and must be claimed when completing the SDLT return by answering 'Yes' at question 9 and inserting Code 32

If the relief was not claimed on the original return, but could have been, an amended return can be made within 12 months of the filing date to rectify the position

When First-Time Buyers' Relief cannot be Claimed

Purchases of non-residential or mixed-use properties (including derelict properties which do not pass the 'suitable for use' as a dwelling test)	✗
Purchases of additional dwellings which are liable to 3% higher rates	✗
Purchases of properties with annexes/granny flats which are capable of independent living and affording full privacy	✗
Purchases of properties which are not intended to be a main residence (such as buy-to-let investment properties) will not qualify for relief	✗
Purchasers who are not individuals, such as companies and trusts	✗
Joint purchasers where not all purchasers qualify as first time-buyers	✗
Spouses/civil partners acting alone but the other spouse/civil partner meets the conditions to render the transaction subject to the 3% higher rates if they were to be party to the transaction	✗

When First-Time Buyers' Relief can be Claimed

Paragraph 1 of Schedule 6ZA FA 2003, provides that **ALL** conditions 1-4, along with the final proviso, must be met in order to be eligible for the relief.

Condition 1: the main subject matter of the transaction consists of a major interest in a single dwelling	✓
Condition 2: the relevant consideration for the transaction (other than any consisting of rent) is not more than £500,000	✓
Condition 3: the purchaser, or (if more than one) each of the purchasers, is a first-time buyer who intends to occupy the purchased dwelling as the purchaser's only or main residence	✓
Condition 4: the transaction is not linked to another land transaction, or, if it is linked, it is only linked to land transactions that are: • an interest in land that is or forms part of the garden or grounds of the purchased dwelling, *or* • an interest in or right over land that subsists for the benefit of the purchased dwelling, or land that is or forms part of the garden or grounds of the purchased dwelling.	✓
Final proviso: relief may not be claimed if it is a higher rates transaction for the purposes of Schedule 4ZA FA 2003	✓

Relief will be withdrawn if a subsequent linked transaction renders the first transaction (on which the relief was claimed) a non-qualifying transaction.[97] The mischief to which this is directed is where, for example, the later transaction takes the relevant consideration above the £500,000 limit, or includes the acquisition of another dwelling.

[97] Para 5 Schedule 6ZA FA 2003

Let's look at each of the conditions above in a bit more detail.

Condition 1: Practical Implications

The main subject-matter of the transaction consists of a major interest in a single dwelling.

Major interest

A major interest is defined as a term absolute which has more than 21 years to run[98]. Therefore, the acquisition of a lease for less than 21 years will not qualify for relief.

Single Dwelling

- There must be an acquisition of a single dwelling. Therefore, purchases of more than one dwelling will not qualify for relief.
- Issues may arise where there is a self-contained part or annex of a building which meets the definition to be treated as a separate dwelling. In such instances, FTB relief will not be available (however, Multiple Dwellings Relief would be available to reduce the SDLT exposure – see later discussion).
- Where the property is in such a state of disrepair to not be classed as 'suitable for use' as a dwelling, the land transaction will not qualify for relief. Instead the transaction will be treated as non-residential and the rates at Table B should be applied. See *P N Bewley Ltd v Revenue and Customs Commissioners [2019] UKFTT 65 (TC)* for discussion on what constitutes 'suitable for use' as a dwelling.

Schedule 6ZA provides the definition of a **dwelling**[99] as follows:

It is used or suitable for use as a single dwelling	✓
It is in the process of being constructed or adapted for such use.	✓
Land that is, or is to be, occupied or enjoyed with a dwelling as a garden or grounds (including any building or structure on that land) is taken to be part of that dwelling.	✓
Land that subsists, or is to subsist, for the benefit of a dwelling is taken to be part of that dwelling.	✓
Off-plan purchases can also count as dwellings where certain conditions are met.	✓
A building or part of a building used for the purposes specified in S116 (2) (which are normally treated as dwellings for SDLT purposes) or (3) FA 2003 (which are not normally treated as dwellings for SDLT purposes) is not regarded as a dwelling for the purposes of the relief.	✓

98 Para 8 Schedule 6ZA FA 2003

99 Para 9 Schedule 6ZA FA 2003

Detailed HMRC guidance

SDLTM00380 – SDLTM00400 (Dated 1 October 2019)	Guidance on what constitutes a dwelling, and guidance on the terms 'suitable for use' and 'in the process of being constructed or adapted for use as a dwelling'.
SDLTM00440 to SDLTM00480 (Dated 25 June 2019)	Guidance on the meaning of garden or grounds for the definition of residential property.
SDLTM00410 – SDLTM00430 (Dated 1 October 2019)	Guidance on how to determine the number of dwellings forming part of a land transaction.

Condition 2: Practical implications

The relevant consideration for the transaction (other than any consisting of rent) is not more than £500,000.

The quantum of the chargeable consideration is calculated using the provisions contained at Schedule 4 FA 2003, typically the money or money's worth given for the transaction.

The aggregate consideration of any linked transactions should be included.

Condition 3: Practical Implications

The purchaser, or (if more than one) each of the purchasers, is a first-time buyer who intends to occupy the purchased dwelling as the purchaser's only or main residence.

There are two important components to this condition:

1. The purchaser, or (if more than one) each of the purchasers, must be a first-time buyer, and
2. They must intend to occupy the purchased dwelling as their only or main residence.

First Time Buyer

The purchaser must be an individual (or the trustee of a bare trust). Relief is not available for persons who are not individuals, e.g. companies and limited liability partnerships (LLP).

The use of the term 'purchaser' is misleading. For SDLT purposes, 'purchaser' is afforded a wide definition that focuses on 'acquiring' as opposed to 'purchasing'[100].

Therefore, the interest held or previously held is not restricted to '**purchases**' and will also include the following:

[100] S43 (4) FA 2003

Inheritances	✓
Gifts	✓
Acquisitions by a financial institution on behalf of a person under an alternative finance scheme	✓

Relief will not be denied by virtue of a previous acquisition if it was acquired by a person acting as a trustee, unless the purchaser was also a beneficiary of the trust and under the terms of the trust acquired a major interest of a dwelling.

Example:

Wendy is purchasing her first home. She inherited 50% in a residential investment property some years ago, which has since been sold.

Wendy will not qualify for relief on the purchase of her first home.

Example:

Xan is purchasing his first home. Some years ago, Xan's parents purchased an investment property in Xan's name by way of a gift in order to prevent the application of the 3% higher rates.

Xan will not qualify for relief on the purchase of his first home.

Example:

Ying is purchasing her first home. Some years ago, Ying acquired an investment property acting in her capacity as trustee of a discretionary trust.

Ying will qualify for relief on the purchase of her new home.

The major interest in a dwelling is not limited to dwellings in England and Northern Ireland, it includes all interests in dwellings worldwide.

Relief will not be precluded by virtue of the purchaser owning or previously owning non-residential or mixed-use property, as long as that property did not include a dwelling. For mixed-use properties, consider:

- whether the dwelling is suitable for use as a dwelling. Derelict properties should not be included
- whether the dwelling is suitably self-contained, capable of independent living and affording sufficient levels of privacy.

Relief will also not be denied if the purchaser has acquired an interest in a dwelling by the grant or assignment of a lease with less than 21 years to run.

Intend to occupy as their only or main residence

There are two further elements within this component:

- Intention
- 'Only or main residence'

All the purchasers must intend to use the dwelling as their only or main residence. A first-time buyer intending to rent out the property will not be entitled to the relief. There could be grey areas, like those buying a property to live in at some time in the future.

Therefore, the intent of use of the purchase should be ascertained from the outset and documented if necessary.

Example:

Zhang is purchasing a buy-to-let property. Zhang has never held an interest in a dwelling (including no previous gifts or inheritances).

Zhang will not qualify for relief.

Example:

Annabelle is purchasing a seaside property. She has never held an interest in a dwelling (including no previous gifts or inheritances). Annabelle lives with her partner and it is intended that the property will be used by the couple as a holiday home.

Annabelle will not qualify for relief.

Example:

Bernard is the trustee of a discretionary trust buying a property for one of the beneficiaries to occupy as their main residence.

Bernard will not qualify for relief.

HMRC accept that it is not necessary that the purchaser must occupy the property immediately following purchase and state:

> *At the effective date of the transaction, there must be a clear intention to occupy the dwelling as the purchaser's only or main residence and the fact that circumstances make it either impossible or impractical to immediately occupy the dwelling do not prevent relief being due.*

Some consideration may be required as to what constitutes a 'main residence'. For this. we refer to *Frost v Feltham (55TC10)* & HMRC Manual SDLTM09812 which includes a helpful list of factors to consider:

- *If the individual is married or in a civil partnership, where does the family spend its time?*
- *If the individual has children, where do they go to school?*
- *At which residence is the individual registered to vote?*
- *Where is the individual's place of work?*
- *How is each residence furnished?*
- *Which address is used for correspondence?*
- *Where is the individual registered with a doctor / dentist?*
- *At which address is the individual's car registered and insured?*
- *Which address is the main residence for council tax?*

Condition 4: Practical Implications

The transaction is not linked to another land transaction.

If the purchase of a dwelling is linked to another transaction then no relief will be available unless the other transaction is the purchase of garden, grounds or interests, or rights in land that subsist for the benefit of the dwelling being acquired.

> ***Example:***
>
> Conrad is purchasing his first home. The dwelling is held by the vendor in their sole name and the surrounding garden and grounds is held by a company in which the vendor holds 100% of the shares.
>
> The purchase is between the same vendor and Conrad, of persons connected with either of them and forms part of a single agreement. Accordingly, both acquisitions will be linked.
>
> Conrad will qualify for relief as the linked transaction is the purchase of the garden and grounds of the purchased dwelling.

Example:

Dana is purchasing her first home. As part of the deal with the vendor, she will also purchase an investment property at a discounted price in six months' time.

Dana will not qualify for relief on the purchase of her first home as it is linked to a non-qualifying property.

Final Proviso: Practical Implications

The legislation provides the final proviso that, even if all four conditions are satisfied, relief may not be claimed if it is a higher-rates transaction for the purposes of Schedule 4ZA FA 2003.

This may seem something of a misnomer: by definition, how can a first-time buyer fall within the additional property purchases provisions? Well, there are a number of different scenarios which can lead to just such an eventuality.

Example:

Ewan, a first-time buyer, wishes to purchase the family's main residence in his sole name. His wife Fiona inherited a property which she currently lets. He is the only purchaser in the transaction and he meets the definition of a first-time buyer.

In this situation, relief would be denied.

This is because spouses are effectively treated as the same person for the 3% surcharge provisions and, therefore, as Fiona owns an additional property, the acquisition of the main residence would attract the higher rate of SDLT.

Accordingly, the only circumstances in which spouses/civil partners can avail of the first-time buyers' relief, in cases where additional properties are held by one of them, is where there is a disposal of a previous main residence in conjunction with the first-time purchase (which was itself intended to be used as a replacement main residence).

There are further situations involving spouses and civil partners which can give rise to the higher rate override.

There can also be issues for beneficiaries of bare trusts and trusts with life or income interest and parents whose minor child has a major interest in a dwelling which is attributed to the parent under the provisions in Schedule 4ZA.

This can be quite a complex area, with a number of nuances and it may be prudent to seek professional advice in cases of doubt.	⚠

First Time Buyers Relief and Shared Ownership

First time buyers' relief can apply to those buying on a shared ownership basis.

Shared ownership buyers (such as those taking a shared ownership lease with a social landlord) have a choice as to how and when to pay SDLT. They can:

- elect to pay SDLT in one lump sum based on the market value of the property. In this case, no further SDLT is payable on future 'staircasing' transactions, *or*
- pay SDLT in stages as and when they purchase each share of the property. This can involve paying SDLT on the net present value of the rents as well as on the up-front price paid.

Initially, relief was only available if the buyer made a market value election. The position was changed with full retrospective effect by the Budget of 29 October 2018 for staircasing transactions to include qualifying properties where no election has been made so that the SDLT is payable in stages.

The relief was extended by the 29 October 2018 Budget to the net present value of the rents.

First Time Buyers' Checklist

RELIEF FOR FIRST-TIME BUYERS CANNOT BE CLAIMED ON:	
Purchases of non-residential or mixed-use properties (including derelict properties which do not pass the 'suitable for use' as a dwelling test)	✕
Purchases of additional dwellings which are liable to 3% higher rates	✕
Purchases of properties with annexes/granny flats which are capable of independent living and afford a sufficient degree of privacy	✕
Purchases of properties which are not intended to be a main residence, i.e. buy-to-let investment properties will not qualify for relief	✕
Purchasers who are not individuals, i.e. companies, LLPs etc	✕
Joint purchasers where not all purchasers qualify as first-time buyers	✕
Spouses/civil partners acting alone but the other spouse/civil partner meets the conditions to render the transaction subject to the 3% higher rates if they were to be party to the transaction	✕
RELIEF FOR FIRST-TIME BUYERS CAN BE CLAIMED IF ALL 4 CONDITIONS AND FINAL PROVISO ARE MET	
Condition 1 - the main subject-matter of the transaction consists of a major interest in a single dwelling	✓
Condition 2 - the relevant consideration for the transaction (other than any consisting of rent) is not more than £500,000	✓
Condition 3 - the purchaser, or (if more than one) each of the purchasers, is a first-time buyer who intends to occupy the purchased dwelling as the purchaser's only or main residence	✓

Condition 4 - the transaction is not linked to another land transaction, or if it is linked, it is only linked to land transactions that are • an interest in land that is or forms part of the garden or grounds of the purchased dwelling, or • an interest in or right over land that subsists for the benefit of the purchased dwelling, or land that is or forms part of the garden or grounds of the purchased dwelling	✓
Final Proviso - relief may not be claimed if it is a higher rates transaction for the purposes of Schedule 4ZA FA 2003	✓

Chapter Twelve
Multiple Dwellings Relief

At a Glance

Multiple Dwellings Relief (MDR)can be claimed on:

- acquisitions of an interest in two or more dwellings
- a mixed-use transaction including at least two dwellings
- acquisitions of an interest in a single dwelling which is linked to the acquisition of an interest in some other dwelling or dwellings.

MDR can significantly reduce the SDLT charge

Interaction with 3% higher rates requires examination in each case.

The legislation provides a **clawback provision**, so that a further return and payment of additional tax will be required where certain conditions are met.

Consider use of Table B rates for purchases of six or more dwellings. Comparison required to determine most tax efficient options.

Introduction

If your client is buying multiple properties in one lot (or in a series of linked transactions), or if there's an annex that's suitable as a dwelling in its own right (such as a granny flat), then multiple dwellings relief is available. This chapter concerns itself with when Multiple Dwellings Relief can be claimed, plus interaction with 3% higher rates and mixed-use properties.

Background

S58D and Schedule 6B provides for relief in the case of transfers involving multiple dwellings.

The explanatory notes to Finance (No 3) Bill 2011 on what is now the Schedule said

> *"Clause 83 and Schedule 22 are designed to strengthen demand for residential property. They will reduce a barrier to investment in residential property, promoting the supply of private rented housing. They do so by reducing the amount of SDLT payable on a purchase of multiple dwellings, so that it is closer to that charged when purchasing those properties singly.*

The measure takes the form of a relief which must be claimed in a land transaction return (or an amendment to such a return). Where a transaction, or a scheme, arrangement or series of linked transactions, includes multiple dwellings, the rate of tax charged in respect of those dwellings is determined by the mean consideration: that is, the total consideration attributable to the dwellings, divided by the number of dwellings."

In practice

- A claim for multiple dwellings relief will, in effect, reduce the SDLT liability to that which would be paid if the properties were purchased separately, i.e. providing access to the multiple use of the lower rate charging bands.
- Where a transaction involves six or more dwellings, it is possible to choose between applying the non-residential rates[101] or making a claim for multiple dwellings relief
- Mixed use cases involving the acquisition of two or more dwellings can claim a mixture of the non-residential rates and include a claim for Multiple Dwellings Relief

The relief is not automatic and must be claimed when completing the SDLT return by answering 'Yes' at question 9 and inserting Code 33	⚠
If the relief was not claimed on the original return but could have been, an amended return can be made within 12 months of the filing date to rectify the position	⚐

When Multiple Dwellings Relief Cannot be Claimed

Purchases which do not involve the purchase of two or more dwellings. Purchases of multiple commercial units only, do not qualify for relief	✕
Purchases of dwellings with annexes or granny flats which are not capable of independent living and affording a sufficient degree of privacy	✕
High value residential property transactions where the 15% charge applies	✕
Where S74 FA 2003 applies - Exercise of collective rights by tenants of flats	✕
Where relief under Schedule 7 (Group Relief) is available	✕
Where relief under Schedule 7A (PAIF Seeding Relief and COACS Seeding Relief) is available	✕
Where relief under Schedule 8 (Charities Relief) is available	✕

[101] S116(7) FA 2003

When Multiple Dwellings Relief can be Claimed

Acquisitions of an interest in two or more dwellings	✓
A mixed-use transaction including at least two dwellings, e.g. the acquisition of a block of residential flats with commercial units	✓
An acquisition of an interest in a single dwelling which is linked to the acquisition of an interest in some other dwelling or dwellings	✓

Calculation

Step 1	Determine the tax that would be chargeable under S55 FA 2003 if the total consideration was divided by the number of dwellings
Step 2	Multiply the amount determined at step 1 by total dwellings
Check	If the amount found at step 2 is less than 1% of the total consideration, then the tax is that 1% amount

Example

Gabriel is purchasing a large Victorian property which contains five residential apartments for £1,000,000.

No relief claimed

Relevant consideration (£)	SDLT rate	SDLT (£)
125,000	3%	3,750
125,000	5%	6,250
675,000	8%	54,000
75,000	13%	9,750
1,000,000		**73,750**

Multiple Dwellings Relief claimed

Relevant consideration (£)	SDLT rate	SDLT (£)
125,000	3%	3,750
75,000	5%	3,750
200,000		**7,500**
X 5 properties (£1,000,000)		**£37,500**
1% of total consideration check		*£10,000*

Result:

The SDLT payable if a claim is made is £37,500. Therefore, the relief provides a saving of £36,250 in this case.

What counts as a dwelling?

Schedule 6B provides the definition of a dwelling[102]

It is used or suitable for use as a single dwelling, See *P N Bewley Ltd v Revenue and Customs Commissioners [2019] UKFTT 65 (TC) for discussion on what constitutes 'suitable for use' a dwelling for these purposes.*	✓
It is in the process of being constructed or adapted for such use.	✓
Land that is, or is to be, occupied or enjoyed with a dwelling as a garden or grounds (including any building or structure on that land) is taken to be part of that dwelling.	✓
land that subsists, or is to subsist, for the benefit of a dwelling is taken to be part of that dwelling	✓
Off-plan purchases can also count as a dwelling where certain conditions are met	✓
A building or part of a building used for the purposes specified in S116 (2) [which are normally treated as dwellings for SDLT purposes] or (3) FA 2003 [which are not normally treated as dwellings for SDLT purposes] is not used as a dwelling for the purposes of the relief	✓

Detailed HMRC guidance

SDLTM00380 – SDLTM00400 (Dated 1 October 2019)	Guidance on what constitutes a dwelling, and guidance on the terms 'suitable for use' and 'in the process of being constructed or adapted for use as a dwelling'.
SDLTM00440 to SDLTM00480 (Dated 25 June 2019)	Guidance on the meaning of garden or grounds for the definition of residential property.
SDLTM00410 – SDLTM00430 (Dated 1 October 2019)	Guidance on how to determine the number of dwellings forming part of a land transaction.

Granny flats/Annexes

Issues can arise with granny flats/annexes to the extent that they qualify as separate dwellings for the purposes of MDR.

HMRC acknowledge in their guidance[103] that annexes are capable of being treated as separate dwellings:

---

[102] Para 7 Schedule 6B FA 2003

[103] SDLTM00410

Sometimes it will be obvious that there are two dwellings, for example 2 flats in a building bought in a single transaction. However, it can sometimes be difficult to discern whether, for example, a 'main house' and 'annex' in the same building should be considered one or two dwellings.

Inevitably, there will be grey areas in the case of a property with an annexe/granny flat, however, a summary of the most determinative factors has been listed below:

Whether or not the other dwelling has all the domestic facilities required for occupation as a dwelling independent of the main dwelling.	✓
Each has a sufficient degree of privacy and security such that two unconnected households could live in the separate parts on a stand-alone basis. (This can be particularly relevant where there is a connecting door or opening between the two parts – see *First Tier Tribunal case of Fiander and Brower v HMRC TC7676*).	✓
The services (such as heating, electricity, gas hot and cold water) are sufficiently capable of independent operation and isolation.	✓
Any legal impediments to selling or letting the other dwelling independently from the main dwelling.	✓

Interaction with 3% higher rates

Where a transaction involves the purchase of two or more separate dwellings, consideration of the conditions set out in Schedule 4ZA in respect of multiple dwelling transactions is required.

There are two separate tests to determine whether the higher rates will be applied depending on how many of the dwellings meet conditions A-C.

Conditions A – C can be summarised as follows:

Condition A is that the chargeable consideration for the purchased dwelling (attributable on a just and reasonable basis) is £40,000 or more.[104]	✓
Condition B is that the purchased dwelling is not subject to a sub-lease which has more than 21 years to run on the day of purchase.[105]	✓
Condition C is that the purchased dwelling is not subsidiary to any of the other purchased dwellings.[106]	✓

[104] Para 5(2) Sch. 4 ZA FA 2003
[105] Para 5(3) Sch. 4 ZA FA 2003
[106] Para 5(4) Sch. 4 ZA FA 2003

Subsidiary dwelling

Condition C is met if the dwelling is not subsidiary to another of the purchased dwellings and was included in the legislation to ensure 'granny flats' did not come within the scope of the higher rates.

The test is two pronged in determining whether a dwelling ('the subsidiary dwelling') is subsidiary to another dwelling ('the principal dwelling').

It must be located in the **same** grounds or building **AND**	✓
The principal dwelling and the garden and grounds attributable to that principal dwelling must be **at least two thirds** of the value of the entire transaction	✓

There can be more than one subsidiary dwelling purchased at the same time as a principal dwelling, but the principal dwelling must always be at least two thirds of the transaction value.

The two separate tests are based on the number of dwellings satisfying conditions A – C

Where at least two of the purchased dwellings meet all conditions A – C[107] and	✓✓
Where only one of the purchased dwellings meet all conditions A – C[108]	✓

Test One - Where at least TWO of the purchased dwellings meet all conditions A – C

Where an individual purchases a major interest in two or more dwellings, the higher rates of SDLT will be applied if at least two of the purchased dwellings meet conditions A, B and C.

Therefore, if there are two or more 'principal' (or 'non-subsidiary dwellings') which are valued at £40,000 or more and are not reversionary on a lease with more than 21 years to run, the higher rates will apply.

It is irrelevant if the individual holds additional properties or if they are replacing a main residence.

Example

Hakan, a property developer, is planning to purchase a block of 15 flats for the total consideration of £1,700,000. Each flat is of a similar value.

Although all the flats are within the same building, all the flats will be considered to be non-subsidiary dwellings by virtue of their valuations. Therefore the 3% higher rates will

---

[107] Para 5 Schedule 4ZA FA 2003

[108] Para 6 Schedule 4ZA FA 2003

apply giving rise to SDLT of £168,750. This is the figure provided when this information is inputted in HMRC's SDLT calculator.

However, S116 (7) FA 2003 specifically provides that where *six or more* dwellings are purchased, they will not be treated as residential property. Accordingly, the rates at Table B (non-residential) should be applied, resulting in the total tax payable of £74,500.

As two or more dwellings are purchased, a claim for Multiple Dwellings Relief should also be considered.

Relevant consideration (£)	SDLT rate	SDLT (£)
113,333	3%	4,000
X 15 properties (£1,700,000)		**£51,000**
1% of total consideration check		*£17,000*

Result:

Therefore, a claim for MDR would result in SDLT payable of £51,000, resulting in a saving of £117,750 compared to the quoted amount on HMRC's calculator.

Test two – Where only one of the purchased dwellings meet all conditions A - C

Where only **one** of the purchased dwellings meets all conditions A – C, the higher rates will only apply if **both** the following conditions are also satisfied:

The purchased dwelling which meets the conditions is not a replacement main residence	✓
At the end of the day that is the effective date of the transaction – the purchaser has a major interest in a dwelling other than one of the purchased dwellings, – that interest has a market value of £40,000 or more, and – that interest is not reversionary on a lease which has an unexpired term of more than 21 years.	✓

Therefore, the consequence of being deemed to be a subsidiary dwelling is that the tests for whether the transaction is a higher rate transaction are applied as if there was, in effect, only one dwelling purchased.

This is confirmed in HMRC's internal guidance at SDLTM09755:

There can be more than one subsidiary dwelling purchased at the same time as a principal dwelling, but the principal dwelling must always be at least two thirds of the transaction value.

Where a principal dwelling is purchased and all the other dwellings purchased are subsidiary dwellings, the tests for whether the transaction is a higher rates transaction are applied as if there was only one dwelling purchased. If the purchase of a principal dwelling is a first property purchase or a replacement of a main residence the higher rates will not apply.

Annexes and granny flats

It is important to note that the fact that an annex or granny flat is treated as a subsidiary dwelling for the purposes of the 3% higher rates (i.e. in effect, one single property), does not preclude MDR from applying, as it will still be treated as a separate dwelling for the purposes of MDR.[109]

Example

Indira and Joe are purchasing a replacement main residence for £1,250,000. The property has a self-contained annex with kitchen, bathroom, bedroom and living space and a lockable door.

The estate agent provided a valuation split of £1,000,000 for the main property and £250,000 for the annex.

The annex is treated as a subsidiary dwelling as the annex is within the same building and the main property is more than two-thirds of the total consideration.

The second test applies as only one property meets conditions A-C. As the property qualifies as replacement main residence, the 3% higher rates will not apply and the SDLT is £68,750 by applying the standard rates at Table A.

On the basis that the annex is capable of independent living and affords a sufficient degree of privacy, the annex will be treated as a separate dwelling for the purposes of MDR.

---

[109] SDLTM09755

Relevant consideration (£)	SDLT rate	SDLT (£)
125,000	0%	Nil
125.000	2%	2,500
375,000	5%	18,750
625,000		21,250
X 2 properties (£1,250,000)		**£42,500**
1% of total consideration check		*£12.500*

Result:

Therefore, a claim for MDR would result in SDLT payable of £42,500, resulting in a saving of £26,250.

Mixed use properties

Where the transaction involves the acquisition of multiple dwellings and non-residential property, two separate calculations must be undertaken to determine the overall SDLT payable.

Example:

Kris is acquiring a property which comprises two ground floor commercial units and five residential flats. The total purchase price is £832,000, with the combined residential value of the property equating to £675,000 and the commercial units valued at £157,000.

Dwellings element and MDR calculation

Relevant consideration (£)	SDLT rate	SDLT (£)
125,000	0%	Nil
10,000	2%	200
135,000		200
X 5 properties (£675,000)		1,000
1% of total consideration check		***£6,750***

Although the MDR calculation provides for an SDLT liability of £1,000, if the aggregate amount of tax found by this method is less than 1% of the total consideration, then the tax is taken to be 1% of the consideration attributable to the dwellings, i.e. in this case, £6,750.

The calculation is prepared on the basis that the standard rates in Table A and not the higher 3% rates apply to the transaction. This is on the basis that the higher rates of SDLT do not apply to mixed use transactions.

It should be noted that HMRC take a different stance at SDLTM29975 in which they apply the 3% higher rates to the calculation.

Non- residential element

The element of the transaction relating to the commercial unit is not a relevant transaction for the purpose of MDR.

The SDLT is calculated based on the total transaction value of £832,000. The total tax on £832,000 should be apportioned to the non-residential consideration of £157,000, i.e. calculate the tax due on the £832,000 (i.e. £31,100 calculated above) then multiply by 18.87% to arrive at the tax due.

This gives rise to SDLT of £5,869.

Result:

Therefore, the total SDLT in relation to the transaction if a claim for MDR is made will be as follows

	SDLT (£)
Residential element with a claim for MDR	6,750
Non-residential element	5,869
	12,619

Adjustments for change of circumstances

It should also be noted that the legislation provides a **clawback provision**, so that a further return and payment of additional tax will be required where:	⚠
relief is claimed under Schedule 6B for a relevant transaction	✓
during a period following the effective date of the transaction(s) (the "relevant period") an event occurs, *and*	✓
if that event had occurred, immediately before the effective date, more tax would have been payable, either because the transaction would not have been a relevant transaction or otherwise then tax is chargeable on the transaction as if the event took place immediately prior to the effective date of the transaction.	✓

For this purpose, "event" includes any change of circumstance or change of plan but does not include an onward sale of individual dwellings.

The HMRC manual[110] states that this provision may be triggered where:

the subject-matter of the transaction ceases to include dwellings (so that the transaction ceases to be a relevant transaction)	✓
the number of dwellings included in the subject-matter of the transaction is reduced (for example by combining smaller dwellings into larger ones).	✓

The **relevant period** is:

- the period ending **three years** after the effective date of the transaction, *or*
- the date on which the purchaser disposes of that dwelling to a person who is not connected with him.

In the case of a transaction substantially performed before completion, the relevant period runs from the date of substantial performance.

The recalculation of the tax due is based on the whole of the consideration given for the subject-matter of the transaction and the number of dwellings following the event, including any dwellings sold on prior to the event.	⚠

[110] SDLTM29965

Multiple Dwellings Relief Checklist

NON-QUALIFYING PURCHASES	
Purchases which do not involve the purchase of two or more dwellings. Purchases of multiple commercial units do not qualify for relief	✗
Purchases of dwellings with annexes or granny flats which are not capable of independent living and affording a sufficient degree of privacy	✗
High value residential property transactions where the 15% charge applies.	✗
Where S74 FA 2003 applies - Exercise of collective rights by tenants of flats	✗
Where relief under Schedule 7 (Group Relief) is available	✗
Where relief under Schedule 7A (PAIF Seeding Relief and COACS Seeding Relief) is available	✗
Where relief under Schedule 8 (Charities Relief) is available	✗
QUALIFYING PURCHASES	
Acquisitions of an interest in two or more dwellings or a mixed-use transaction including at least two dwellings, e.g. the acquisition of a block of residential flats with or without commercial units	✓
An acquisition of an interest in a single dwelling which is linked to the acquisition of an interest in some other dwelling or dwellings	✓
INDICATIVE FACTORS OF A SINGLE DWELLING	
Does the dwelling have all the domestic facilities required for independent living? • **Sleeping area** • **Kitchen** • **Bathroom** • **Living area**	✓
Does the dwelling have an independent or separate entrance?	✓

Does the dwelling afford a sufficient degree of privacy and security for independent living? **In the case of adjoining properties:** • **is there a lockable door?** • **Is the door sufficiently sound and fireproof?**	✓
Does the dwelling have services (such as heating, electricity, gas, hot and cold water) which are sufficiently capable of independent operation and isolation without entering another property to control?	✓
Are there any legal impediments which inhibit use as a separate dwelling?	✓
Is the dwelling separately assessed for council tax?	✓
Has the dwelling been documented as a separate dwelling in any estate agents marketing material?	✓
Does the dwelling have its own separate postal address for utilities and suchlike?	✓

Chapter Thirteen
Leases – Schedule 17A

At a Glance

SDLT is payable on both premiums and rent paid in respect of the grant of a lease.

Premiums are taxed in accordance with Table A or B in the normal way.

A special formula is applied to calculate the chargeable consideration in respect of rents.

There are special rules for the continuation of a lease after its fixed term and leases for indefinite terms.

The SDLT implications associated with leases can be complex and care is required in non-standard cases as the HMRC SDLT calculator does not deal with anomalies.

Relief can be claimed for the leaseback element of a sale and leaseback provided certain conditions are met.

Introduction

This chapter addresses the main issues arising in relation to leases and highlights where care is required.

What is chargeable

SDLT is payable on land transactions, which are defined as 'any acquisition of a chargeable interest[111]'. A lease is an interest in land and is therefore a chargeable interest[112].

The distinction between a lease and a licence is important as a licence to use or occupy land and a tenancy at will, are exempt interests and are not liable to SDLT[113].

Leases are subject to SDLT on

Any premium paid for the grant of a lease	✓
Any rent payable over the term of the lease at the net present value (NPV)	✓

[111] S43 FA 2003

[112] S48(1)(a) FA 2003

[113] S48 (2) FA 2003

Where both a premium and rent is payable for the grant of a lease, the tax due on the two elements of consideration will be calculated separately and added together to determine the total SDLT payable.

The following are not counted as chargeable consideration for the grant of a lease

An undertaking by the tenant to repair, maintain or insure the let premises	✕
A tenant's undertaking to pay in respect of services, repairs, maintenance, insurance or management costs	✕
Any other tenant's obligation that does not affect the open market rent	✕
Any rent or performance guarantee	✕
Penal rent	✕
Costs borne by a tenant exercising a statutory right to be granted a new lease	✕
Any other obligation by a tenant to bear the landlord's reasonable costs incidental on the grant of a lease	✕
An obligation under a lease, on its termination, to transfer to the landlord payment entitlements under the scheme of income support for farmers in respect of land subject to the scheme (Council Reg 73/2009/EC refers).	✕
Reverse premiums do not count as chargeable consideration	✕

Premiums

What counts as a premium?

Any consideration other than rent	✓
Rent paid before the lease is granted may be taxable as a premium	✓
Rent deposits	✓

Lease premiums are taxed in accordance with either Table A (entirely residential) or Table B (mixed use or commercial) in the normal way, i.e.

Table A

Relevant consideration	SDLT rate	Higher SDLT rate
Up to £125,000	0%	3%
£125,001 - £250,000	2%	5%
£250,001 - £925,000	5%	8%
£925,001 - £1,500,000	10%	13%
£1,500,001 +	12%	15%

Table B

Relevant consideration	SDLT rate
Up to £150,000	0%
£150,001 - £250,000	2%
£250,001 +	5%

Rent

Step 1 – Determine the rent payable

Rent is not defined for SDLT purposes and HMRC take the view that it takes its ordinary meaning - i.e. a periodic payment for the use of land/property and it will be a question of fact as to whether a payment is rent.

What does not count as rent

Rent does not include consideration payable before a new lease is granted (but may be taxed as a premium).	✕
Service charges as long as they are • provided for in the lease as a separate figure *or* • expressed in the lease as part of an inclusive rent payment and apportioned on a just and reasonable basis.	✕

Rent payable

Rent reviews	
Years 1 - 5	Actual rent payable used to calculate NPV
Years 5 +	Assumed to be at an annual amount equal to the highest amount of rent payable for any consecutive 12-month period in the first five years.[114]
Term includes part year	
Part year	The annual rent should be apportioned to the number of days in the part year. The part year will always fall at the end of the lease for the purposes of calculating net present value.
Variable or uncertain rent	
Contingent	Any contingency in years 1 - 5 is taken to have occurred
Uncertain or unascertained	Reasonable estimate used for years 1 -5 (e.g. where rentals are subject to a review or are based on turnover)

---

[114] Paragraph 7, Schedule 17A FA 2003

Step 2 - Calculation of Net Present Value (NPV)

SDLT is charged on any chargeable consideration consisting of rent as a percentage of the net present value of the rent payable over the term of the lease.

The net present value (V) of the rent payable over the term of the lease is calculated by applying the formula contained at Schedule 5 FA 2003[115].

$$V = \sum_{i=1}^{n} \frac{r_i}{(1+T)^i}$$

r_i is the rent payable in respect of year 'i'

i is the particular year for which the calculation is to be performed (a calculation being required for each year)

n is the term of the lease

T is the temporal discount rate (currently 3.5%)

Example

A lease is granted for 3 years with annual rent of £200,000. The NPV is calculated as follows

Year	Rent	Calculation	NPV
1	200,000	200,000/(1+0.035)	193,237
2	200,000	$200,000/(1+0.035)^2$	186,702
3	200,000	$200,000/(1+0.035)^3$	180,389
			560,327

The HMRC SDLT calculator will calculate the NPV and resultant SDLT payable in basic scenarios.

However, care is needed, for example, when the term of the lease includes part years or when overlap relief is to be claimed etc. Manual calculations of the NPV are preferable when dealing with non-standard transactions.

[115] Para 3 Schedule 5 FA 2003

Step 3 – Appliable Rates

Having calculated the NPV, the SDLT is calculated in accordance with the rates contained at Table A or B specific for leases.

Table A - Residential

NPV	SDLT rate
Up to £125,000	0%
£125,001 +	1%

Table B – Non-Residential or Mixed-Use

NPV	SDLT rate
Up to £150,000	0%
£150,001 - £5,000,000	1%
£5,000,000 +	2%

Term of lease and Continuation

Leases that Continue After a Fixed Term

Treatment of Original Lease

Where a lease continues after the expiry of its fixed term, it is in the first place treated as extended in yearly increments. Any additional tax is not due until 30 days after the end of each one-year period of extension[116].

From 1 March 2019, where a return is required, because the lease becomes notifiable for the first time, this must be made within 14 days of the end of the first year of holding over.

Example

- A 10-year non-residential lease expired on 31 March 2020
- The tenant remained in occupation whilst they negotiated a new lease with the landlord
- Annual rent was £60,000 per annum
- The lease was originally granted on 1 April 2010 and notified on 20 April 2010
- NPV of the rent was originally returned as £498,996 and SDLT of £3,489 was paid

[116] Para 3 Schedule 17A FA 2003

On 1 April 2020 (the day after the original express term ended), the lease is treated as being for one year longer than its express term, that is a lease for 11 years granted on 1 April 2010.

The NPV of the rent for this notional 11-year lease is £540,093 and SDLT of £3,900 is due. However, as £3,489 has already been paid, the net additional SDLT due is £411.

If the new lease is not agreed by 31 March 2021, a second notional lease will be treated as being granted on 1 April 2021, with a term of 12 years granted on 1 April 2010.

This process is repeated until the new lease is granted (or terminated).

Treatment of New Lease

Where a new lease is subsequently granted (of the same or substantially the same premises) within one year of the expiry of the original lease (or of any one-year extension), the new lease is treated as if it were granted on the day after the expiry of the original lease (or of the previous one-year's extension)[117]. The above deeming provisions are therefore disapplied in the year that the new lease is granted.

Example:

Building on the above example, a new lease is subsequently agreed and granted on 1 June 2020 for a term of 10 years.

The new lease is treated as if it were granted on 1 April 2020 and therefore for the purposes of calculating the SPV, the term of the lease will be 10 years and 2months (1 April 2020 – 30 May 2030).

However, these rules do not apply where a backdated lease is granted within one year (or extended year) of a tenant holding over. In these circumstances, under paragraph 9A of Schedule 17A the term of the new lease is treated for SDLT purposes as beginning on the date on which it is expressed to begin (i.e. on or immediately after the contractual termination date of the old lease).

Any rent payable in respect of the period between the expiry of the original lease and the actual date of grant of the new lease is eligible for relief in the same way as for `overlap relief' (discussed in further detail below).

---

[117] Para 3A Schedule 17A 2003

> ***Example:***
>
> Following the same facts of the examples above, except that the lease granted on 1 June 2020 expresses the start date of the lease to be 1 April 2020 ending on 31 March 2030.
>
> The notional lease for 11 years granted on 1 April 2010 is still required to be reported, as above with the additional SDLT of £411 being payable.
>
> However, for the purposes of calculating the NPV of the new lease, the rent for the first year will not be included in the calculation so as to prevent a double tax charge on this amount. This will be reportable before the reporting of the notional lease above.

Treatment of Leases for Indefinite Term

Leases for an indefinite period are treated in a similar manner to leases which continue after a fixed term[118], such as:

- initially as a lease for a fixed term of a year
- if the lease continues after that term, as a lease for a fixed term of two years and
- if the lease continues thereafter, as a lease for a fixed term of three years

and so on until the term is fixed or a new lease is granted.

Treatment of Successive Linked Leases

Where successive leases are granted or treated as granted (at the same or different times) of the same or substantially the same premises and the grants are linked transactions (between the same parties or persons connected with them as part of a single scheme, arrangement or series of transactions), the leases are treated as a single lease.

The aggregated lease is treated as if it were granted at the time of the grant of the first lease in the series for a term equal to the aggregate of all the terms and for the total rent payable under all the leases.

Where the leases are granted at different times, the tax chargeable on the new lease in excess of the tax chargeable on the old lease is payable within 14 days or 30 days of the effective date of the new lease.

Extending the Term of a Lease

Surrender and Re-grant

Where a lease is granted in consideration of the surrender of an existing lease between the same parties, the grant of the new lease does not count as chargeable consideration

---

[118] Para 4 Schedule 17A FA 2003

for the surrender and the surrender does not count as chargeable consideration for the grant of the new lease, so paragraph 5 of Schedule 4 FA 2003 (exchanges) is disapplied.

Where the new lease is of the same or substantially the same premises and the existing lease was subject to SDLT when granted, **'overlap' relief** will apply so that the rent payable under the new lease for the same period as the existing lease will be reduced by the amount of rent that would have been payable for that period under the existing lease, in assessing SDLT on the rent under the new lease[119].

Example

Original lease granted on 1 April 2019 for three years with annual rent of £200,000. The NPV is calculated as follows

Year	Rent	Calculation	NPV
1	200,000	200,000/(1+0.035)	193,237
2	200,000	$200,000/(1+0.035)^2$	186,702
3	200,000	$200,000/(1+0.035)^3$	180,389
			560,327

The lease is surrendered and regranted on 1 October 2020 for a further five years with the annual rent remaining at £200,000 pa. The NPV (taking into account overlap relief) is calculated as follows

Year	Rent	Calculation	NPV
1	0	0/(1+0.035)	0
2	100,000	$100,000/(1+0.035)^2$	93,351
3	200,000	$200,000/(1+0.035)^3$	180,389
4	200,000	$200,000/(1+0.035)^4$	174,288
5	200,000	$200,000/(1+0.035)^5$	168,395
			616,423

[119] Paragraph 9, Schedule 17A FA 2003

Variation of a Lease

Increase of Rent in First Five Years

Where a lease is varied to increase the rent in the first five years of the lease (but outside the terms of the lease, such that the variation does not fall to be included in any calculation of NPV) the variation is treated as if it were the grant of a new lease in consideration of the additional rent payable[120].

The rules for abnormal rent increases after the fifth year were repealed by FA 2013 so that such increases are no longer treated as a grant of a new lease.

Reduction of rent or term or other variation of lease

Reduction of rent or other variation

Where a lease is varied so that the rent is reduced, the variation is treated as the acquisition of a chargeable interest by the tenant[121].

As the tenant already has a major interest (the lease), a land transaction return is only required if the variation is for chargeable consideration exceeding the relevant threshold.

Where any consideration in money or money's worth (other than an increase in rent) is given by the tenant for any variation of a lease, other than a variation of the amount of the rent or of the term of the lease, the variation is treated as an acquisition of a chargeable interest by the tenant.

Reduction of term

Where a lease is varied so as to reduce the term, this is treated as the acquisition of a chargeable interest by the lessor[122].

This is the acquisition of a major interest since the tenant is relinquishing part of their major interest (the lease). If the landlord gives chargeable consideration of £40,000 or more to the tenant, a land transaction return will be required. Otherwise the transaction does not have to be notified.

Assignment of a Lease

The assignment of a lease is generally chargeable in the same way that a freehold transfer is chargeable and therefore subject to the rates at Table A or B, as appropriate.

---

[120] Para 13 Schedule 17A FA 2003

[121] Para 15A (1) Schedule 17A FA 2003

[122] Para15A (2) Schedule 17A FA 2003

However, where the grant of a lease is exempt by virtue of the availability of the following reliefs, the first assignment of the lease that is not exempt by virtue of any of these reliefs, is treated as if it were granted for the unexpired term at the current rent.

S57A (sale and leaseback)	✓
Schedule 7 (group, reconstruction or acquisition relief)	✓
Schedule 7A (PAIF seeding relief and COACS seeding relief)	✓
S66 (transfers involving public bodies)	✓
Schedule 8 (charities relief)	✓
Regulations made under section 123(3) (reproducing exemptions from stamp duty)	✓
Paragraphs 6 and 8 of Schedule 61 to the Finance Act 2009 (alternative finance investment bond)	✓

Agreements for Lease

The application of the provisions in relation to contracts (S44 FA 2003) are modified in relation to agreements for lease, so that, where the agreement is substantially performed prior to the grant of the lease, it is treated as the grant of a notional lease for SDLT purposes.

If the lease is then granted pursuant to the agreement, the actual lease and notional lease are treated as a single lease[123]:

Granted on the date that the agreement for lease was substantially performed	✓
For a term beginning with the date of substantial performance and ending on the expiry of the actual lease	✓
In consideration of the total rent payable over the term of the single lease (and any premium given).	✓

The notional and actual leases are treated as linked for the purposes of section 81A and, if there is any additional tax to pay, it is the lessee under the actual lease who must submit a further return and pay the tax.

In other respects, the actual lease is disregarded for SDLT purposes and in many practical cases the grant of the actual lease will not trigger either a tax payment or a notification requirement.

If the agreement is not 'substantially performed' before the lease itself is concluded, the agreement is treated as part of the same transaction as the lease and the effective date will be that of the lease itself.

[123] Para 12A Schedule 17A FA 2003

Linked Transactions

Where leases of two or more properties are negotiated as a single bargain between the same or connected parties, the transactions will be treated as linked for SDLT purposes. If the special provisions for successive leases do not apply (see above), the calculation of the NPV is modified[124] and the chargeable consideration is aggregated for the purposes of applying SDLT rates and thresholds.

HMRC provide worked examples of the calculation at SDLTM17050-SDLTM17055.

Notification

The grant of a lease is notifiable if it is for seven or more years and any chargeable consideration is £40,000 or more, or the relevant rent is £1,000 or more[125].	✓
The assignment or surrender of a lease is notifiable if the lease was originally granted for seven or more years and the chargeable consideration is £40,000 or more, or the relevant rent is £1,000 or more[126]	✓
The grant, assignment or surrender of a lease for less than seven years is not notifiable unless the chargeable consideration exceeds the nil rate threshold[127]	✓
Continuation of a lease after its fixed term	✓

Sale and Leaseback arrangements

Provided certain conditions are met, the leaseback element of a sale and leaseback arrangement is exempted from the charge to SDLT by section 57A FA 2003.

The sale element of the transaction remains chargeable on its market value (as the transaction is, in effect, an exchange).

Application

A "sale and leaseback" arrangement means an arrangement under which[128]—

- *A* transfers or grants to *B* a major interest in land (the "sale"), and
- out of that interest *B* grants a lease to *A* (the "leaseback").

---

[124] Para 2(5) & (6) Schedule 5 FA 2003
[125] S77 & S77A (3) FA 2003
[126] S77 & S77A (4) FA 2003
[127] S77 & S77 (5) –(6) FA 2003
[128] S57A (2) FA 2003

The leaseback must therefore be to the person who sold the major interest.

In addition, the following specific conditions must ALL be satisfied[129]:

That the sale transaction is entered into wholly or partly in consideration of the leaseback transaction being entered into	✓
That the only other consideration (if any) for the sale is the payment of money or the assumption, satisfaction or release of a debt (or both)	✓
That the sale is not a transfer of rights within the meaning of S45A (contract providing for conveyance to third party: effect of transfer of rights) or a pre-completion transaction within the meaning of Schedule 2A (transactions entered into before completion of contract)	✓
Where A and B are both bodies corporate at the effective date of the leaseback transaction, that they are not members of the same group for the purposes of group relief (see paragraph 1 of Schedule 7) at that date	✓

Where the above conditions are satisfied and the sale and lease-back are between the same parties, relief will be available to ensure that only the initial sale element will be chargeable to SDLT.

HMRC have confirmed[130] that the chargeable consideration for the sale leg will depend upon whether there was a written agreement, at the time of the sale, for the leaseback leg to be entered into. If there was, the chargeable consideration for the sale leg should take this encumbrance into account and can therefore be regarded as having a nominal value depending on the specific leaseback arrangement.

If there is no such agreement, the chargeable consideration for the sale leg will relate to the unencumbered interest in land.

It is therefore very important to have a written agreement in place documenting the leaseback arrangement so as to reduce the SDLT exposure on such transactions.	⚐

The relief is not automatic and must be claimed by completing the land transaction return by answering yes at question 9 to show a relief is being claimed and inserting Code 28 ('Other relief')	⚠
If the relief was not claimed on the original return but could have been, an amended return can be made within 12 months of the filing date to rectify the position	⚐

[129] S57A (3) FA 2003

[130] SDLTM16040

Chapter Fourteen
Partnership Transactions: Schedule 15

At a Glance

To fall within Schedule 15, a partnership must carry on a 'business' with the view to make profit.

A jointly held property portfolio can fall within these provisions provided there is a sufficient level of active involvement in the management of the portfolio.

The legislation distinguishes between ordinary and special partnership transactions.

Ordinary transactions apply the normal rules to determine the chargeable consideration.

The normal rules are disapplied and instead specific formulas are used to determine chargeable consideration for 'special' partnership transactions.

Introduction

Schedule 15 details how SDLT will apply to partnership transactions. For the Schedule to apply, a partnership must exist, which requires the carrying on of a 'business' with the view to make profit.

This chapter does not seek to cover the full application of Schedule 15, but identifies the key provisions likely to be relevant to conveyancers in practice, namely land transfers to and from partnerships.

Background

Schedule 15 FA 2003 provides special rules to be applied to transactions involving partnerships and is split into three parts

Part 1	General provisions
Part 2	Ordinary partnership transactions
Part 3	Transactions to which special provisions apply

General Provisions

What is a partnership

A partnership for the purposes of SDLT is defined as[131]:

a partnership within the Partnership Act 1890	✓
a limited partnership registered under the Limited Partnerships Act 1907	✓
a limited liability partnership formed under the Limited Liability Partnerships Act 2000 or the Limited Liability Partnerships Act (Northern Ireland) 2002 or	✓
a firm or entity of a similar character to any of the above formed under the law of a country or territory outside the United Kingdom	✓

A partnership is treated as the same partnership notwithstanding a change in membership if any person who was a member before the change remains a member after the change.[132]

Requirement to carry on a 'business'

In determining whether or not a partnership exists, HMRC refer to S1(1) of the Partnership Act 1890, which provides as follows:

> *`Partnership is the relation which subsists between persons carrying on a business in common with a view of profit'.*

Accordingly, a partnership will only exist if the entity carries on a 'business'. It is important to note the distinction between 'business' and 'trade', the latter being a more stringent test of commercial activity applied or the purposes of other tax reliefs.

Where an entity does not carry on a business there will not be a partnership and the partnership provisions in Schedule 15 will not apply, even if the parties are bound by a partnership deed.	⚠

In most cases it will be easily ascertainable if an entity is carrying on a business so there is no doubt that a partnership exists.

Jointly held property portfolios

There is a grey area in relation to the joint ownership of property portfolios.

131 Para 1 Schedule 15 FA 2003
132 Para 3 Schedule 15 FA 2003

HMRC manual PIM1030 provides a helpful summary of HMRC's view of jointly owned property in which they accept that investment portfolios held jointly with the requisite level of business activity can constitute a partnership for these purposes.

Moreover, the case of *Elizabeth Moyne Ramsay v HMRC TC 1871* although not specially dealing with the SDLT partnership provisions, provides helpful guidance on what constitutes a property investment business (The case dealt with what constitutes a 'business' for the purposes of CGT incorporation relief).

The evidence provided in this case was that the Ramsays spent circa 20 hours a week on tasks related to the property, such as maintenance, collecting rents, and cleaning the flats after tenants left.

It was held that this level of activity amounted to more than passive receipt of rents, and therefore constituted a business for these purposes.

Ordinary Partnership Provisions

Ordinary partnership transactions - transactions entered into as purchaser by or on behalf of the members of a partnership other than transactions subject to the special partnership provisions	✓
Calculation of chargeable consideration – apply normal principles contained at Schedule 4 FA 2003	✓
All partners are responsible for any SDLT obligations	✓
All partners are jointly and severally liable for any SDLT, interest and penalties imposed (except those who became partner after the effective date)	✓

Special Partnership Provisions

The special rules are contained in Part 3 of Schedule 15 FA 2003 and apply to certain transactions involving the transfer of:

a chargeable interest to a partnership by a partner or connected person[133]	✓
an interest in a partnership. Generally, changes in partners or in partnership shares do not give rise to a charge to SDLT unless the partnership is a property investment partnership[134].	✓
a chargeable interest from a partnership to any of its partners, or person connected with them[135]	✓

[133] Paragraph 10-11 Schedule 15 FA 2003

[134] Paragraph 14 Schedule 15 FA 2003

[135] Paragraph 18-23 Schedule 15 FA 2003

Transfers – include: • the grant or creation of a chargeable interest, • the variation of a chargeable interest, and • the surrender, release or renunciation of a chargeable interest	✓
Calculation of chargeable consideration - computed on the market value of the partnership property by reference to the change in the proportion of the interest held before and after the transaction. Neither actual consideration nor any related debt is taken into account.	✓

The remainder of this chapter considers the implications of land transfers to and from partnerships.

Transfer of a Chargeable Interest to a Partnership by a Partner or Connected Person

Application

These special rules will apply where a chargeable interest is transferred

to a partnership by a partner	✓
to a partnership by a person in return for an interest in the partnership	✓
to a partnership by a person connected with either of the above	✓

Connected persons are defined for SDLT purposes by reference to S1122 CTA 2010.

The provisions apply whether the transfer is in connection with the formation of the partnership or is a transfer to an existing partnership.

Calculation of chargeable consideration

Para 10 provides that any actual consideration provided for the transfer is disregarded, and the consideration deemed to have been payable for the transfer will be calculated in accordance with the following formula:

MV x (100 – SLP) %

Where 'MV' is the market value of the interests transferred and 'SLP' is the sum of the lower proportions.

The legislation details five steps to determine the SLP,[136] the process of which can be quite complex. In cases of doubt, it may be prudent to seek professional advice.

[136] Paragraph 12 Schedule 15 FA 2003

Step 1	**Identify the relevant owner or owners** A person is a relevant owner if – immediately before the transaction, he was entitled to a proportion of the chargeable interest, and – immediately after the transaction, he is a partner or connected with a partner
Step 2	**For each relevant owner, identify the corresponding partner or partners** A person is a corresponding partner in relation to a relevant owner if, immediately after the transaction – he is a partner, and – he is the relevant owner (or is an individual connected with the relevant owner)
Step 3	**For each relevant owner, find the proportion of the chargeable interest to which he was entitled immediately before the transaction** Apportion that proportion between any one or more of the relevant owner's corresponding partners.
Step 4	**Find the lower proportion for each person who is a corresponding partner in relation to one or more relevant owners** The lower proportion is – the proportion of the chargeable interest attributable to the partner, or – if lower, the partner's partnership share immediately after the transaction The proportion of the chargeable interest attributable to the partner is – if he is a corresponding partner in relation to only one relevant owner, the proportion (if any) of the chargeable interest apportioned to him (at Step Three) in respect of that owner – if he is a corresponding partner in relation to more than one relevant owner, the sum of the proportions (if any) of the chargeable interest apportioned to him (at Step Three) in respect of each of those owners
Step 5	**Add together the lower proportions of each person who is a corresponding partner in relation to one or more relevant owners** The result is the sum of the lower proportions.

Example:

Lottie, Marion and Nina are partners in a solicitors practice, with a profit-sharing ratio of 20%, 40% and 40% respectively. Lottie wishes to transfer a property which she owns entirely to the partnership. The property is valued at £200,000.

Lottie, Marion and Nina are not connected by virtue of S1122 CTA 2010.

Step 1: Lottie is the relevant owner

Step 2: Lottie is the corresponding partner

Step 3: Lottie was entitled to 100% of the property

Step 4: Lottie is entitled to 20% of the property following the transfer

Step 5: SLP is 20%

The chargeable consideration is calculated as follows

£200,000 x (100 – 20) % = £160,000

Essentially, the chargeable consideration equates to the amount of the property that Lottie has relinquished an interest in.

Example:

The above facts remain the same, except that Lottie and Marion are connected for the purposes of S1122 CTA 2010.

In this scenario Lottie and Marion are the corresponding partners for the purposes of step 2 and the SLP at step 5 is 60% taking into account Marion's interest. Therefore, the chargeable consideration in this case is calculated as £200,000 x (100 – 60) % = £80,000.

A property-investment partnership can make an election to disapply this treatment and instead pay tax by reference to the market value of the whole chargeable interest transferred[137].

[137] Paragraph 12A Schedule 15 FA 2003

<table>
<tr><th colspan="2">Anti-avoidance provisions</th></tr>
<tr><td>Para 17<ul><li>Where relief is obtained on the transfer of property by a partner or a person connected with a partner to a partnership and</li><li>At the time of the transfer there were arrangements in place for a subsequent transfer of interests in the partnership</li><li>SDLT is charged on the subsequent transfer by reference to the market value of the property and the proportion of interest transferred</li></ul></td><td>⚠</td></tr>
<tr><td>Para 17A<ul><li>Where there is a transfer of land into a partnership and</li><li>Within three years of the transfer there is a withdrawal of money or money's worth other than income profit or a loan is repaid (in relation to the transferor or a person connected with him)</li><li>The withdrawal or repayment is treated as a chargeable transaction and</li><li>The chargeable consideration is taken to be the withdrawal or repayment up to the market value of the chargeable interest transferred, less any tax previously chargeable.</li></ul>This can lead to a potential double tax charge where one partner contributes land and the other partner contributes a cash equalisation payment which is then paid out to the partner contributing the land.</td><td>⚠</td></tr>
</table>

Transfer of a chargeable interest from a partnership to any of its partners, or person connected with them

Application

These special rules will apply where a chargeable interest is transferred

From a partnership to a person who is or has been one of the partners	✓
From a partnership to a person connected with a person who is or has been one of the partners	✓

Connected persons are defined for SDLT purposes by reference to S1122 CTA 2010.

Calculation of chargeable consideration

Para 18 provides that any actual consideration provided for the transfer is disregarded, and the consideration deemed to have been payable for the transfer will be calculated in accordance with the following formula:

MV x (100 – SLP) %

Where 'MV' is the market value of the interests transferred and 'SLP' is the sum of the lower proportions.

The legislation details five steps to determine the SLP,[138] the process of which can be quite complex. In cases of doubt, it is recommended that professional advice is sought.

Step 1	**Identify the relevant owner or owners** A person is a relevant owner if – immediately after the transaction, he is entitled to a proportion of the chargeable interest, and – immediately before the transaction, he was a partner or connected with a partner
Step 2	**For each relevant owner, identify the corresponding partner or partners** A person is a corresponding partner in relation to a relevant owner if, immediately before the transaction – he was a partner, and – he was the relevant owner (or was an individual connected with the relevant owner)
Step 3	**For each relevant owner, find the proportion of the chargeable interest to which he is entitled immediately after the transaction** Apportion that proportion between any one or more of the relevant owner's corresponding partners.
Step 4	**Find the lower proportion for each person who is a corresponding partner in relation to one or more relevant owners** The lower proportion is – the proportion of the chargeable interest attributable to the partner, or – if lower, the partnership share attributable to the partner The proportion of the chargeable interest attributable to the partner is – if he is a corresponding partner in relation to only one relevant owner, the proportion (if any) of the chargeable interest apportioned to him (at Step Three) in respect of that owner – if he is a corresponding partner in relation to more than one relevant owner, the sum of the proportions (if any) of the chargeable interest apportioned to him (at Step Three) in respect of each of those owners
Step 5	**Add together the lower proportions of each person who is a corresponding partner in relation to one or more relevant owners** The result is the sum of the lower proportions.

[138] Paragraph 20 Schedule 15 FA 2003

Where the SLP is calculated to be 100, the deemed chargeable consideration for the transaction will be Nil (as the multiplier applied to the market value will be zero).

This will be the case where the land is transferred to any of the partners or persons connected to them. It will also apply on an incorporation of a partnership, where the partners (or persons connected with them) hold the entire shareholding in the limited company.

***Example*:**

Ophelia, Pat and Quincy are partners in a solicitors' practice, with a profit-sharing ratio of 20%, 40% and 40% respectively. The partners wish to transfer a partnership property to Ophelia. The property is valued at £200,000.

Ophelia, Pat and Quincy are not connected by virtue of S1122 CTA 2010.

Step 1: Ophelia is the relevant owner

Step 2: Ophelia is the corresponding partner

Step 3: Ophelia is entitled to 100% of the property

Step 4: Ophelia's partnership share is 20%

Step 5: SLP is 20%

The chargeable consideration is calculated as follows

£200,000 x (100 – 20) % = £160,000

Essentially, the chargeable consideration equates to the amount of the property that Ophelia has acquired an interest in.

Example:

The above facts remain the same except that Ophelia and Pat are connected for the purposes of S1122 CTA 2010.

In this scenario Ophelia and Pat are the corresponding partners for the purposes of step 2 and the SLP at step 5 is 60% taking into account Pat's interest. Therefore, the chargeable consideration in this case is calculated as £200,000 x (100 – 60) % = £80,000.

Interaction with S53 FA 2003

S53 FA 2003 provides that the market value of the property should be substituted as chargeable consideration in the circumstance where a company is the purchaser and the vendor is connected with the company.

Where a transaction is within both S53 FA 2003 and Para 10 or Para 18 Schedule 15 FA 2003, HMRC accept that the legislation within Schedule 15 will take priority to determine the consideration[139].

Example:

Rory, Sandra and Tom are partners in a solicitors' practice, with a profit-sharing ratio of 20%, 40% and 40% respectively. The partners wish to transfer their trading premises to RST Ltd as part of the incorporation of the solicitor practice business. The property is valued at £200,000. The individual interests in RST Ltd will mirror the profit-sharing ratio in the existing partnership.

Rory, Sandra and Tom are not connected by virtue of S1122 CTA 2010.

Step 1: Rory. Sandra and Tom are the relevant owners

Step 2: Rory. Sandra and Tom are the corresponding partners

Step 3: RST Limited is entitled to 100% of the property

Step 4: Rory: 20%, Sandra: 40% and Tom:40%

Step 5: SLP is 100

The chargeable consideration is calculated as follows

£200,000 x (100 – 100) % = Nil

[139] SDLTM34170

Individuals could be tempted to convert a sole trader business to a partnership by bringing in a family partner (as an intermediate step) before subsequently transferring properties on incorporation, to eliminate the SDLT exposure. However, such arrangements are particularly vulnerable to the general SDLT anti-avoidance rule at S75A FA 2003 (discussed in further detail at chapter 15). If HMRC can demonstrate that the 'partnership' was inserted to avoid an SDLT charge, then this transaction would be set aside and SDLT would be charged on the market value under S53 FA 2003.	

Chapter Fifteen
Anti-Avoidance

At a Glance

There are a number of targeted anti-avoidance provisions including 'linked transactions.'

Where the linked transactions provisions apply, the total aggregated consideration must be taken into account when calculating the SDLT payable.

The SDLT legislation also includes a general anti-avoidance provision at S75A FA 2003, which is drafted widely with no motive defence or time barring for application.

There are also a series of anti-avoidance case law on the matter.

Other non-SDLT specific tax anti-avoidance provisions should be considered

- GAAR (Part 5 FA 2013)
- DOTAS (Part 7 FA 2004)
- Follower notices and accelerated payments (Part 4 FA 2014)

Introduction

The SDLT legislation contains a number of targeted anti-avoidance provisions and a general anti-avoidance provision. There are also non-specific SDLT anti-avoidance provisions that can apply.

In this chapter, we'll look at some of these in more detail.

The application of the anti-avoidance provisions can be complex and it may be prudent to seek professional advice, in cases of doubt.

Linked transactions

Background

This anti-avoidance provision was introduced to ensure that transactions carried out at the same time or as part of a wider arrangement between the same vendor and purchaser (or persons connected with them) are treated as linked, even if they are documented independently. Essentially, HMRC were concerned that independent documentation was being used in order to reduce the SDLT payable.

What are linked transactions

Legislative definition	
Form part of a single scheme, arrangement or series of transactions	✓
Between the same vendor and purchaser	✓
Or between persons connected with the vendor or purchaser	✓
'Connected persons' is defined at S1122 CTA 2010	✓
HMRC practice	
Single scheme or arrangement - where the transactions are documented separately	✓
Single scheme or arrangement - where the land is split and purchased by separate individuals/entities who are connected	✓
Series of transactions - where a discount has been secured because of the other transaction(s)	✓
Series of transactions - one transaction cannot complete without the other	✓

As you can appreciate, this is a very wide definition and therefore can catch most transactions between the same vendor and purchaser (or persons connected with them).

Essentially, the question to be answered is, 'Are the transactions part of a single deal or a series of interrelated transactions?'

What will not be linked transactions

HMRC practice	
Single scheme or arrangement – where a transaction has not been artificially separated by way of the legal documentation or by substituting a different (connected) vendor or purchaser.	✕
Series of transactions – where there is no prior agreement or option to enter into further transactions.	✕
Series of transactions - Where no special price or discount has been secured.	✕
Series of transactions – where the terms of the particular transaction are in all material respects identical to what they would have been had the other transaction(s) not occurred.	✕

Calculation

The consequence of transactions being linked is that the appropriate rates must be applied to the aggregate consideration.

Therefore, the resultant SDLT will be higher than if the transactions are counted individually as they lose the benefit of multiple lower threshold bands.

Calculation

Type of linked transaction	Method
Single scheme or arrangement	**Step 1** - calculate the amount of tax due on the total chargeable consideration for all the transactions **Step 2** - apportion total tax due between the transactions, in proportion to their share of the total chargeable consideration
Series of transactions	**Step 1** - calculate the amount of tax due on the total chargeable consideration for all the transactions to date, at the rates in force at the time of that transaction **Step 2** - apportion total tax due to each transaction in proportion to its share of the total chargeable consideration **Step 3** – Consider previous linked transactions to determine if additional tax is payable and additional reporting requirements

Applicable rates

Type of property	Rates applicable
All linked transactions consist of entirely **residential** property	Rates at **Table A** applied to aggregate consideration
All linked transactions consist of entirely **non-residential** property	Rates at **Table B** applied to aggregate consideration
Linked transactions include both residential and non-residential property	Rates at **Table B** applied to aggregate consideration

General Anti-Avoidance Provisions

The impact of the main SDLT anti-avoidance provision (S75A FA 2003), anti-avoidance case law and the general anti-abuse rule (GAAR) must be considered in more complex transactions. Appropriate professional advice should be obtained in cases of doubt.

The SDLT GAAR - S75A FA 2003

S75A FA 2003 is the main anti-avoidance provision and is drafted extremely widely with no motive test nor time limit for having effect.

HMRC quote Lord Hodge in the Supreme Court Judgment in *Project Blue Ltd v Commissioners for Her Majesty's Revenue and Customs [2018]* in their internal guidance[140] UKSC 30 in relation to the application of S75A FA 2003:

> *"it is sufficient for the operation of [Section 75A] that tax avoidance, in the sense of a reduced liability or no liability to SDLT, resulted from the series of transactions which the parties put in place, whatever their motive for transacting in that manner"*

Therefore, where there has been a reduction in the final SDLT liability as a result of a number of other transactions, S75A can be invoked even if the transactions are carried out for commercial reasons with no underlying tax avoidance motive. In simple terms, it seems that it is simply enough to have a reduction in liability for the provision to apply.

It applies where:

one person (V) disposes of a chargeable interest in land and another person (P) acquires either it or an interest deriving from it	✓
a number of transactions (which can include non-land transactions) are involved in connection with the disposal and acquisition	✓
the sum of the SDLT payable in respect of these transactions is less than the amount which would be payable on a notional transaction effecting the acquisition of V's chargeable interest by P on its disposal by V	✓

In such circumstances, SDLT is chargeable on the greater of the amount given by any one person under the transactions or received by V (or a person connected with V) by way of consideration for those transactions.

HMRC detailed internal manual guidance can be found at **SDLTM09050 – SDLTM09370.**

Other considerations

The General Anti-Avoidance Rule ('GAAR') was introduced by Part 5 FA 2013 with effect from 17 July 2013, and its scope includes SDLT.	✓
The disclosure of tax avoidance scheme (DOTAS) rules in Part 7 FA 2004 requires a disclosure to be made to HMRC concerning certain planning arrangements involving SDLT.	✓
HMRC has also obtained further powers, through the ability to issue follower notices and accelerated payment notices in Part 4 FA 2014 and their scope includes SDLT. The powers are quite extensive and the right of the taxpayer to appeal is limited.	✓

[140] SDLTM09090

More Books by Law Brief Publishing

A selection of our other titles available now:-

'Covid-19, Homeworking and the Law – The Essential Guide to Employment and GDPR Issues' by Forbes Solicitors
'Covid-19, Force Majeure and Frustration of Contracts – The Essential Guide' by Keith Markham
'Covid-19 and Criminal Law – The Essential Guide' by Ramya Nagesh
'Covid-19 and Family Law in England and Wales – The Essential Guide' by Safda Mahmood
'Covid-19 and the Implications for Planning Law – The Essential Guide' by Bob Mc Geady & Meyric Lewis
'Covid-19, Residential Property, Equity Release and Enfranchisement – The Essential Guide' by Paul Sams and Louise Uphill
'Covid-19, Brexit and the Law of Commercial Leases – The Essential Guide' by Mark Shelton
'Covid-19 and the Law Relating to Food in the UK and Republic of Ireland – The Essential Guide' by Ian Thomas
'A Practical Guide to the General Data Protection Regulation (GDPR) – 2nd Edition' by Keith Markham
'Ellis on Credit Hire – Sixth Edition' by Aidan Ellis & Tim Kevan
'A Practical Guide to Working with Litigants in Person and McKenzie Friends in Family Cases' by Stuart Barlow
'Protecting Unregistered Brands: A Practical Guide to the Law of Passing Off' by Lorna Brazell
'A Practical Guide to Secondary Liability and Joint Enterprise Post-Jogee' by Joanne Cecil & James Mehigan
'A Practical Guide to the Pre-Action RTA Claims Protocol for Personal Injury Lawyers' by Antonia Ford
'A Practical Guide to Neighbour Disputes and the Law' by Alexander Walsh
'A Practical Guide to Forfeiture of Leases' by Mark Shelton
'A Practical Guide to Coercive Control for Legal Practitioners and Victims' by Rachel Horman
'A Practical Guide to Rights Over Airspace and Subsoil' by Daniel Gatty
'Tackling Disclosure in the Criminal Courts – A Practitioner's Guide' by Narita Bahra QC & Don Ramble

'A Practical Guide to the Law of Driverless Cars – Second Edition' by Alex Glassbrook, Emma Northey & Scarlett Milligan
'A Practical Guide to TOLATA Claims' by Greg Williams
'Artificial Intelligence – The Practical Legal Issues' by John Buyers
'A Practical Guide to the Law of Prescription in Scotland' by Andrew Foyle
'A Practical Guide to the Construction and Rectification of Wills and Trust Instruments' by Edward Hewitt
'A Practical Guide to the Law of Bullying and Harassment in the Workplace' by Philip Hyland
'How to Be a Freelance Solicitor: A Practical Guide to the SRA-Regulated Freelance Solicitor Model' by Paul Bennett
'A Practical Guide to Prison Injury Claims' by Malcolm Johnson
'A Practical Guide to the Small Claims Track' by Dominic Bright
'A Practical Guide to Advising Clients at the Police Station' by Colin Stephen McKeown-Beaumont
'A Practical Guide to Antisocial Behaviour Injunctions' by Iain Wightwick
'Practical Mediation: A Guide for Mediators, Advocates, Advisers, Lawyers, and Students in Civil, Commercial, Business, Property, Workplace, and Employment Cases' by Jonathan Dingle with John Sephton
'The Mini-Pupillage Workbook' by David Boyle
'A Practical Guide to Crofting Law' by Brian Inkster
'A Practical Guide to Spousal Maintenance' by Liz Cowell
'A Practical Guide to the Law of Domain Names and Cybersquatting' by Andrew Clemson
'A Practical Guide to the Law of Gender Pay Gap Reporting' by Harini Iyengar
'A Practical Guide to the Rights of Grandparents in Children Proceedings' by Stuart Barlow
'NHS Whistleblowing and the Law' by Joseph England
'Employment Law and the Gig Economy' by Nigel Mackay & Annie Powell
'A Practical Guide to Noise Induced Hearing Loss (NIHL) Claims' by Andrew Mckie, Ian Skeate, Gareth McAloon
'An Introduction to Beauty Negligence Claims – A Practical Guide for the Personal Injury Practitioner' by Greg Almond
'Intercompany Agreements for Transfer Pricing Compliance' by Paul Sutton
'Zen and the Art of Mediation' by Martin Plowman
'A Practical Guide to the SRA Principles, Individual and Law Firm Codes of Conduct 2019 – What Every Law Firm Needs to Know' by Paul Bennett
'A Practical Guide to Adoption for Family Lawyers' by Graham Pegg
'A Practical Guide to Industrial Disease Claims' by Andrew Mckie & Ian Skeate
'A Practical Guide to Redundancy' by Philip Hyland

'A Practical Guide to Vicarious Liability' by Mariel Irvine
'A Practical Guide to Applications for Landlord's Consent and Variation of Leases' by Mark Shelton
'A Practical Guide to Relief from Sanctions Post-Mitchell and Denton' by Peter Causton
'A Practical Guide to Equity Release for Advisors' by Paul Sams
'A Practical Guide to Unlawful Eviction and Harassment' by Stephanie Lovegrove
'A Practical Guide to the Law Relating to Food' by Ian Thomas
'A Practical Guide to Financial Services Claims' by Chris Hegarty
'The Law of Houses in Multiple Occupation: A Practical Guide to HMO Proceedings' by Julian Hunt
'A Practical Guide to Unlawful Eviction and Harassment' by Stephanie Lovegrove
'A Practical Guide to Solicitor and Client Costs' by Robin Dunne
'Occupiers, Highways and Defective Premises Claims: A Practical Guide Post-Jackson – 2nd Edition' by Andrew Mckie
'A Practical Guide to Financial Ombudsman Service Claims' by Adam Temple & Robert Scrivenor
'A Practical Guide to Advising Schools on Employment Law' by Jonathan Holden
'A Practical Guide to Running Housing Disrepair and Cavity Wall Claims: 2nd Edition' by Andrew Mckie & Ian Skeate
'A Practical Guide to Holiday Sickness Claims – 2nd Edition' by Andrew Mckie & Ian Skeate
'Arguments and Tactics for Personal Injury and Clinical Negligence Claims' by Dorian Williams
'A Practical Guide to QOCS and Fundamental Dishonesty' by James Bentley
'A Practical Guide to Drone Law' by Rufus Ballaster, Andrew Firman, Eleanor Clot
'A Practical Guide to Compliance for Personal Injury Firms Working With Claims Management Companies' by Paul Bennett
'A Practical Guide to the Landlord and Tenant Act 1954: Commercial Tenancies' by Richard Hayes & David Sawtell
'A Practical Guide to Dog Law for Owners and Others' by Andrea Pitt
'RTA Allegations of Fraud in a Post-Jackson Era: The Handbook – 2nd Edition' by Andrew Mckie
'RTA Personal Injury Claims: A Practical Guide Post-Jackson' by Andrew Mckie
'On Experts: CPR35 for Lawyers and Experts' by David Boyle
'An Introduction to Personal Injury Law' by David Boyle
'A Practical Guide to Chronic Pain Claims' by Pankaj Madan
'A Practical Guide to Claims Arising from Fatal Accidents' by James Patience
'A Practical Guide to Subtle Brain Injury Claims' by Pankaj Madan

These books and more are available to order online direct from the publisher at www.lawbriefpublishing.com, where you can also read free sample chapters. For any queries, contact us on 0844 587 2383 or mail@lawbriefpublishing.com.

Our books are also usually in stock at www.amazon.co.uk with free next day delivery for Prime members, and at good legal bookshops such as Wildy & Sons.

We are regularly launching new books in our series of practical day-to-day practitioners' guides. Visit our website and join our free newsletter to be kept informed and to receive special offers, free chapters, etc.

You can also follow us on Twitter at www.twitter.com/lawbriefpub.